# REFLECTIONS PART I

*Kenny Harmon*

**SAD PAPAW**

**Reflections Part I**
Copyright © 2023 by Kenny Harmon

ISBN: 978-1639458059 (hc)
ISBN: 978-1639457595 (sc)
ISBN: 978-1639457601 (e)

All rights reserved. No part of this publication may be reproduced, distributed, or transmitted in any form or by any means, including photocopying, recording, or other electronic or mechanical methods, without the prior written permission of the publisher, except in the case brief quotations embodied in critical reviews and other noncommercial uses permitted by copyright law.

The views expressed in this book are solely those of the author and do not necessarily reflect the views of the publisher, and the publisher hereby disclaims any responsibility for them.

Writers' Branding
(877) 608-6550
www.writersbranding.com
media@writersbranding.com

# Pacific Book Review

"They say to see into our future, we must first look into our past. The future is determined by the lessons we learned from the past, which is true on both a personal and social level. History is one of the great teachers of the world. To be able to learn from the mistakes of the past and determine what our future can be is one of life's greatest opportunities, and sometimes the best way to understand our own personal past is to see it through the lens of the historical events which we lived through.

This is the lesson and theme author Kenny Harmon brings to the table in his book Reflections Part 1. Written in response to the viral story of "Sad Paw," the author reflects on the life of the Harmon family, tracing the history of the family into the past, and showcasing the impact that both the family had on society, and which society had on the family in turn. From the war-torn European theater of WWII to the athletes and celebrities who would take the world by storm, the author showcases how these eras helped shape the course of the family over the years.

Immediately what stuck out to me, as a reader, was the balance the author highlighted between the history of the family itself, to the worldwide history which helped define the path his family took. The author was very detailed in his writing on this topic, and had a great sense of imagery in the writing, which brought these eras to life on the pages for readers. The depth of heart which went into the book, and the attention to pop culture detail, as well as the history of the past century, really cultivated a compelling and engaging narrative.

For those who enjoy non-fiction reads, memoirs, biographies and history books, this is the perfect read. The honesty and depth the author brought to his personal family's history, and the captivating knowledge these eras held together, make the book feel vibrant and alive on the pages. Overall, the quick pace of the book itself allows enough room for the readers to be able to come back to the book time-and-time again, as interest in the history and pop culture aspects of the book meshed with the author and his family's personal history."

– Jack Chambers

# Hollywood Book Reviews

"Kenny Harmon's Reflections, Part I is a heartfelt memoir comprising the triumphs and struggles of Kenny Harmon and the lessons he learned since his teenage days.

Hermann was a famous name of the ancient German lineage and those called by it were fortunate to explore as far west as the Mississippi River, with one of them founding the first English-speaking settlement west of the Allegheny Mountains in 1745. Some of the family members settled in Pennsylvania, while others moved to the Shenandoah Valley, and North Carolina, after which they changed the spelling of the Hermann name to Harman or Harmon.

On March 16th, 2016, Kenny Harmon became an internet sensation after a family cookout that went wrong. His granddaughter Kelsey noticed his pitiful look and proceeded to scoff at the others with his photo as he bit on his burger. The image had the caption, "Dinner with Papaw tonight… he made 12 burgers for all 6 grandkids, and I'm the only one who showed. love him." A firestorm of empathy broke out on the internet, and in less than 24 hours, major media houses had the waves saturated with his name. Kenny got the chance to host a second cookout, and to his surprise, multitudes flowed from all over the world to share some love with him as they reflected on the importance of periodically checking on loved ones.

Harmon's account accentuates the importance of unity, love, and devotion in the family setup. He has offered inspiring lessons that households can emulate to prevail over the challenges life throws at them. As a reader, I was greatly inspired by his story and couldn't get enough of the historical occurrences shared, which included the sighting of the first UFO in 1952, the release of the first telephone answering machine in 1957, and the introduction of the first TV dinner in 1953.

Kenny Harmon's Reflections, Part I has been beautifully written and edited. The author is a master storyteller, mentor, and motivator who honors dedication and sacrifice. I loved his enthusiasm in sharing his rich family's history and can't wait to get my hands on Part II of his awe-inspiring introspections. I highly recommend this book to readers of all ages."

– Ephantus M.

*This book is dedicated to all Military Verterans
and*

*In Loving Memory of
Bill and Wanda Harmon
(Paw-Paw & Nanny)*

# Table of Contents

Chapter 1: Part 1: The Origins of Hermann/Harman/Harmon ..... 1
    Part 2: The Long Journey ..................................................... 2
    Part 3: The Long Journey ..................................................... 3
    Part 4: The Long Journey ..................................................... 9
    Part 5: Hairbreadth Escapes ............................................... 12
    Part 6: The Battle of Warfield and the Capture of Jane Wily ............................................................................... 13
    Part 7: Daniel Harman son of Capt. Henry "Old Skygusty" Harman From the annals of Tazewell County, Virginia ................................................... 18
    Part 8: Mathias "Tice" Harman The Founding of Harman's Station ............................................................. 19

Chapter 2: Across the Miles ................................................................. 28

Chapter 3: Part 1: A Timeline of Sport's History ......................... 42
    Part 2: Baseball Days ......................................................... 42
    Part 3: What's In a Name? ................................................. 57
    Part 4: National Football League (NFL) Kicks Off .... 63
    Part 5: What's In A Name? ................................................ 69
    Part 6: Oklahoma Sooners ................................................ 70

Chapter 4: Part 1: Kenny, Cars… and Cruisin'............................78
    Part 2:  Little Bit of History................................81
    Part 3:  Making Drag Racing History....................82
Chapter 5: Part 1: Music and Movies that Changed a Generation ....97
    Part 2:  Rockin' in the '50s and '60s........................108
    Part 3:  The Birth of Rock n' Roll..........................112
    Part 4:  Making of Motown ...................................117
Chapter 6: Part 1: America at War World War II - War for the
              Pacific..........................................................127
    Part 2:  Battle of Wake Island.................................130
    Part 3:  Battle of the Coral Sea ...............................130
    Part 4:  Battle of Midway.......................................131
    Part 5:  Battle at Guadalcanal.................................132
    Part 6:  Battle of Saipan .........................................133
    Part 7:  Battle of the Philippine Sea........................135
    Part 8:  Battle of Peleliu.........................................136
    Part 9:  Battle of Angaur .......................................137
    Part 10: Battle of Leyte Gulf....................................138
    Part 11: Battle of Iwo Jima.......................................138
    Part 12: Battle of Okinawa ......................................140
    Part 13: The Korean War .........................................150
    Part 14: The Vietnam War .......................................152
Chapter 7: Harmans Move West ..............................................162

## About the Author

Kenny Harmon is a retired ironworker from Dibble, OK. He was a 4th generation farmer of watermelons & numerous other crops in the Dibble/Blanchard Okla communities. The story of Sad Papaw began March 16th, 2016 when his granddaughter Kelsey Harmon posted a tweet about her Papaw cooking a dozen burgers for six grandkids but she was the only one to be at his house.

Ten days later on March 26th, Kenny had a cookout in which everyone was invited to a Sad Papaw cookout. More than two thousand people from at least 28 different states came. Folks from New York, Virginia, California, Washington, Canada & a woman representing a media company from Australia! Since the big cookout we have had cookouts for Veterans & the homeless.

*The tweet that started it all...*

 **kelsey**
@kelssseyharmon

dinner with papaw tonight... 🖤 he made 12 burgers for all 6 grandkids and I'm the only one who showed. 😢 love him

# Chapter 1

## Part 1 The Origins of Hermann/Harman/Harmon

The Harman Surname. The surname Harman is the Frankish (French) analog of the ancient German name Hermann (Herman), composed of the root words "hari," meaning "army" and "mann," meaning "man." The English analog of the name today is Harmon. It is a name of ancient lineage and was mentioned by the Roman Historian Tacitus c. 56-117 A.D., who, in his "Histories" written nearly 2,000 years ago, told of the victory of Arminius (Hermann), Chief of the German tribe Cherusci, over the Roman legions of Publius Quinctilius Varus in the Teutoburgiensis Saltus — the Teutoburg Forest. The Battle of the Teutoberger Wald in 9 A.D. was one of the pivotal battles of world history and Arminius' victory is credited with halting the expansion of the Roman Empire under Augustus Caesar at the Rhine frontier. It forever prevented the complete subjugation of the Germans by the Romans. And, although Roman legions later won stunning victories over one or another German, Gaulic or Celtic army, the Romans never succeeded in subduing the German culture, or retaining hegemony over the German tribes. Augustus Caesar's plan to move the German frontier to the Elbe was never realized. The battle was a master stroke of military strategy. Arminius, a military commander, was leader of the German tribe of the Cherusci who were allied to the Romans. But Varus' harsh, despotic and arbitrary rule led Arminius to plan a rebellion against Roman rule. He persuaded Varus to lead his three legions and auxiliary troops into the Teutoburg Forest in the late summer of 9 A.D. Arminius was at the head of the rear guard with his Cherusci troops. There, in the forest near modern Detmold, Roman supply wagons mired down and Roman troops broke formation as Arminius had foreseen. At a signal, German guerrillas stationed in advance by Arminius attacked, the German recuits deserted, and Arminius and his rear guard fell upon the unsuspecting Romans. The Romans, their formations in disaray, were surrounded and cut down by the Germans. Varus vainly tried to march west to safety, but by the second day, the Germans had annihilated all the Roman cavalry. By the third day, some 20,000 Roman infantry had perished and Varus, humiliated, committed suicide. It is said that Augustus agonized over the defeat by Arminius for the remainder of his life and was heard often to cry in anguish from his quarters at night: "Varus! Give me back my legions!" Hans Bahlow's "Dictionary of German Names," published in English translation by the Max Kade Institute for German-American studies at the University of Wisconsin, Madison, indicates that Herrmann is the preferred spelling today in Bavaria, while Hoermann is the Austrian spelling and Hiermann the Low German spelling. Harmen is a famous and ancient German personal name. Notable German Harmans (Hermanns) have included Hermann Billung, duke of the Saxons about 950 and Landgrave Hermann of Thuringia, patron of Middle High German poets around 1200. It is mentioned in Goethe's long poem "Hermann and Dorothea" and was revived in popularity as a family name by Klopstock and the Romantics around 1800.

## Part 2

## The Long Journey

Johann Michael Hermann was born in the district of Ludwigsburg, Germany in 1669. Johann married Kundigunda Christina Regis. Christina gave birth to Heinrich Adam Hermann in 1700 in Mannheim, Wurttenberg, Germany. Heinrich Adam married Louisa Katrina Mathias.

In 1726 Adam and Louisa and 2-year-old Henry Adam Jr. departed Germany for America. Shortly after boarding the ship "Charlotte", the vessel docked at the Isle of Mann, located between Great Britain and Ireland. While on the Isle Louisa gave birth to Heinrich Henry. The voyage from Great Britain to America normally was 6 to 7 weeks in the mid- 1720's. Henrich Adam and Louisa would have 11 more children after reaching America. There were 7 Hermann brothers that made the journey to America. Henrich Adam, Johann Jacob (my 5th great grandfather), Valintine, Mathis, George, Daniel and John. The Hermanns changed the spelling to Harman or Harmon after becoming Americans. The Hermanns/Harmans/Harmons would become great frontiers men that explored as far west as the Mississippi River. Heinrich Adam Harman founded the first English-speaking settlement west of the Allegheny Mountains in 1745!

Part 3

The Long Journey

By Emory L. Hamilton

From the unpublished manuscript, Indian Atrocities Along the Clinch, Powell and Holston Rivers. Walter Crockett, County Lieutenant of Militia for Montgomery Co., VA, wrote to Governor Edmund Randolph, on February 16, 1789, (1), saying:

    I take this opportunity to write to you by Captain Sayers, who is going to Richmond on business of his own, to inform you of the state of our frontiers in this county. There has been several of our hunters from the frontier down the Sandy River forty or fifty miles below the settlement on Bluestone on the Clinch, and discovered fresh signs of several parties of Indians, one of the hunters is a brother (2) to Henry Harman, that had the skirmish with them late in the fall, (November 12, 1788) when he and his two sons behaved like heroes, they came immediately in, and warned the frontier settlements, and has applied to me to send out spies. They say that if there was four Scouts that they could confide in, they would endeavor to plant corn this spring, and stay the summer. Otherwise, Bluestone settlement will break up, and of course the settlement on the head of Clinch will not stand long. I expect as soon as the winter breaks up, that the Indians will commit hostilities on some part of the frontiers of this county the ensuing spring, but God only knows the event. Whatever orders your Excellency and shall be punctually obeyed.

    This family of Harmans were of German origin, Adam Heinrich Hermann emigrating to America in 1726, with a brief stop over the Isle of Man, where Henry Harman of this sketch was born. (3) Seven Harman brothers emigrated from Germany together, Jacob, Valentine, Mathias, George, Daniel, John, and Heinrich Adam. They first stopped off in Pennsylvania, then emigrated to the Shenandoah Valley and some on into North Carolina. At least three of these brothers settled in Southwest Virginia, namely, Heinrich Adam, Valentine and Jacob. They were living in the New River German settlement, the first settlement ever made west of the Alleghenies on the "Western Waters", and were living there prior to 1745. In 1749 Moravian Missionaries conducted the first recorded religious services in Southwest Virginia in the home of Jacob Harman, and Dr. Thomas Walker mentions stopping at the home of Harman on his memorable exploration trip in 1750. Of these three brothers, Valentine and Jacob were both killed by Indians on New River. Valentine was killed on Sinking Creek in what is now Giles Co., VA. In a land suit filed in the High Court of Chancery in Augusta Co., on the 23rd of July, 1807, Taylor vs Harman, (4) Mathias Harman, nephew of the slain Valentine, says: Valentine was killed by the Indians on New River and at the same time his (Mathias') brother, Daniel Harman and Andrew Moser were taken prisoner. Daniel made his escape, but Andrew was held prisoner.

On the 30th of June, 1808, Daniel Harman, deposes, in the same land suit, saying: In 1757, Valentine was killed in my presence less than a foot away from me, and I was taken prisoner. Valentine Harman, who was slain left a widow Mary Harman, but no children.

Jacob Harman lived on Neck Creek in what is now Pulaski Co., VA, on what is known as Spring Dale Farm. In 1757, he, his wife, and one of his sons were murdered by the Indians.

The Harmans of this sketch are the descendants of Heinrich Adam Hermann who emigrated from Germany, who married Louisa Katrina, October 8, 1723. Louisa Katrina died March 18, 1749. The children of this marriage were: [1] Adam Harman, the eldest, born in Germany in 1724; [2] Henry Harman born on the Isle of Man in 1726; [3] George Harman, 1727 - 1749; [4] Daniel Harman, born Pennsylvania, 1729; [5] Mathias Harman, born near Strausburg, VA, in 1736; [6] Christina Harman, who married Jeremiah Pate, and lived on Little River in Montgomery Co., VA; [7] Catherine Harman who married Ulrich Richards in Rowan Co., NC; [8] Phillipina Harman, who died in 1751; [9] Valentine Harman who settled on the upper Clinch River in 1771, and moved to Lincoln Co., KY, about 1775, and was a member of the Henderson Legislature at Boonesboro in May, 1775; [10] A daughter, name unknown, married a Mr. Looney; [11] Jacob Harman, perhaps the Jacob who settled in Tazewell Co., VA in 1771.

The sons of old Heinrich Adam Hermann, the German emigrant, became great hunters and Indian fighters. While most of them were great hunters, one in particular became one of the noted Long Hunters. It is hard to determine just which son this was, but evidence points to the youngest who was Jacob.

Henry, the second son of Heinrich Adam, owned land in North Carolina, Giles and Tazewell counties in Virginia. Sometime in the 1750s, he was married to Anna Wilborn of the Moravian settlement in North Carolina, and died at his home at "Holly Brook" on Kimberlin Creek in present day Bland Co., VA, in 1822. In 1789, he and his son, Mathias, founded Harman's Station in Kentucky. There is much evidence in the records to prove the great prowess of the Harmans as hunters and Indian fighters. In another land suit in the High Court of Chancery of Augusta Co., Wynn vs Inglish heirs, (5) it is stated: that Henry Harman was in the habit of collecting the men and fighting the

Indians. In a land dispute case filed in Augusta (6), Samuel Walker states on May 30, 1805, that he came to the head of Clinch in 1771 and met Valentine Harman. In the same suit Mathias and Daniel Harman, brothers of Henry, state that they were on the land in dispute on a hunting trip in 1760. This statement proves that the Harmans were familiar with the country at the head of Clinch and Bluestone Rivers long before they made actual settlement in the area. In the Minutes of the Court of Montgomery County for May 26, 1790, is found this entry:

Inhabitants of Bluestone ordered to show cause why they should not work on that part of the road between Rocky Gap and the head of Clinch. The following were appointed overseers of the road, among whom was Captain Henry Harman.

Details of the fight between Henry Harman and the Indians are taken from Bickley's History of Tazewell County, with the correct date added.

On the 12th of November, 1788, Henry Harman, and his two sons, George and Mathias, and George Draper left the settlement, to engage in a Bear hunt on Tug River. They were provided with pack horses, independent of those used for riding, and on which were to be brought in the game. The country in which their hunt was to take place, was penetrated by the "warpath" leading to and from the Ohio river; but as it was late in the season they did not expect to meet with Indians.

Arriving at the hunting grounds in the early part of the evening, they stopped and built their camp; a work executed generally by the old man, who might be said to be particular in having it constructed to his own taste. George and Mathias loaded, and put their guns in order, and started to the woods, to look for sign, and perchance kill a buck for the evening repast, while Draper busied himself in hobbling and caring for the horses.

In a short time, George returned with the startling intelligence of Indians! He had found a camp but a short distance from their own, in which partly consumed sticks were still burning. They could not, of course, be at any considerable distance, and might now be concealed near them, watching their every movement. George, while at the camp, had made a rapid search for sign, and found a pair of leggins, which the old man believed the leggins to have been taken from the body of Capt. Moore after the Moore massacre. Now old Mr. Harman, was a type of frontiersman, in some things, and particularly that remarkable self- possession, which is so often to be met with in new countries, where dangers are ever in the path of the settler. So taking a seat on the ground, he began to interrogate his son on the dimensions, appearance, etc., of the camp. When he had fully satisfied himself, he remarked, that, "there must be from five to seven Indians", and that they must pack up and hurry back to the settlements, to prevent, if possible, the Indians from doing mischief; and, said he, "if we fall in with them, we must fight them."

Mathias was immediately called in, and the horses repacked. Mr. Harman and Draper, now began to load their guns, when the old man observing Draper, laboring under what is known to hunters as the "Buck Ague", being that state of excitement, which causes excessive trembling, remarked to him, "My son, I fear you cannot fight."

The plan was now agreed upon, which was, that Mr. Harman and Draper should lead the way, the pack horses follow them, and Mathias and George bring up the rear. After they had started, Draper remarked to Mr. Harman that he would go ahead, as he could see better than Mr. Harman, and that he would keep a sharp lookout. It is highly probable that he was cogitating a plan of escape, as he had not gone far before he declared he saw the Indians, which proved not to be true.

Proceeding a short distance further, he suddenly wheeled his horse about, at the same time crying out, "Yonder they are - behind that log." As a liar is not to be believed when he speaks the truth, so Mr. Draper was not believed this time. Mr. Harman rode on, while a large dog, he had with him, ran up to the log and reared himself upon it, showing no sign of the presence of Indians. At this second, a sheet of fire and smoke from the Indians' rifles, completely concealed the log from view, for Draper had really spoken the truth.

Before the smoke had cleared away, Mr. Harman and his sons were dismounted, while Draper had fled with all the speed of a swift horse. There were seven of the Indians, only four of whom had guns; the rest being armed with bows and arrows, tomahawks and scalping knives. As soon as they fired, they rushed on Mr. Harman, who fell back to where his two sons stood ready to meet the Indians.

They immediately surrounded the three white men, who had formed a triangle, each man looking out, or, what would have been, with men enough a hollow square. The old gentleman bid Mathias to reserve his fire, while himself and George fired, wounding, as it would seem, two of the Indians. George was a lame man, from having had white-swelling in his childhood, and after firing a few rounds, the Indians noticed his limping, and one who had fired at him, rushed upon him thinking him wounded. George saw the fatal tomahawk raised, and drawing back his gun, prepared to meet it. When the Indian had got within striking distance, George let down upon his head with the gun, which brought him to the ground; he soon recovered, and made at him again, half-bent and head foremost, George sprang up and jumped across him, which brought the Indian to his knees. Feeling for his own knife, and not getting hold of it, he seized the Indians' and plunged it deep into his side. Mathias struck him on the head with a tomahawk, and finished the work with him.

Two Indians had attacked the old man with bows, and were maneuvering around him, to get clear fire at his left breast. The Harmans, to a man, wore their bullet pouches on the left side, and with this and his arm he so completely shielded his breast, that the Indians did not fire till they saw the old gentleman's gun nearly loaded again, when one fired on him, and struck his elbow near the joint, cutting one of the principal arteries. In a second more, the fearful string was heard to vibrate, and an arrow entered Mr. Harman's breast and lodged against a rib. He had by this time loaded his gun, and was raising it to his face to shoot one of the Indians, when the stream of blood from the wounded artery flew into the pan, and so soiled his gun that it was impossible to make it fire. Raising his gun, however, had the effect to drive back the Indians, who retreated to where the others stood with their guns empty.

Mathias, who had remained an almost inactive spectator, now asked permission to fire, which the old man granted. The Indian at whom he fired appeared to be the chief, and was standing under a large beech tree. At the report of the rifle, the Indian fell, throwing his tomahawk high among the limbs of the tree under which he stood.

Seeing two of their number lying dead upon the ground, and two more badly wounded, they immediately made off; passing by Draper, who had left his horse, and concealed himself behind a log.

As soon as the Indians retreated, the old man fell back on the ground exhausted and fainting from the loss of blood. The wounded arm being tied up and his face washed in cold water, soon restored him. The first words he uttered were, "We've whipped them, give me my pipe." This was furnished him, and he took a whiff, while the boys scalped one of the Indians.

When Draper saw the Indians pass him, he stealthily crept from his hiding place, and pushed on for the settlement, where he reported the whole party murdered. The people assembled and started soon the following morning to bury them; but they had not gone far before they met Mr. Harman, and his sons, in too good condition to need burying.

Upon the tree, under which the chief was killed, is roughly carved an Indian, a bow and a gun, commemorative of the fight. The arrows which were shot into Mr. Harman, are in possession of some of his descendants. David E. Johnston in his History of the Middle New River Settlements gives a ballad which he says was composed by Captain Henry Harman, herein inserted to show the correct date and add interest to the details of this story.

## Capt. Henry Harman's Battle Song

Come all ye bold heroes whose hearts flow with courage,

With respect pay attention to a bloody fray. Fought by Captain Harman and valiant sons,
With the murdering Shawnees they met on the way. The battle was fought on the twelfth of November, Seventeen hundred and eighty-eight.
Where God of his mercy stood by those brave heroes, Or they must have yielded to a dismal fate.
Oh! Nothing would do this bold Henry Harman, But down to the Tug River without more delay, With valiant sons and their noble rifles,
Intending a number of bears to slay.
They camped on Tug River with pleasing contentment, Till the sign of blood thirsty Shawnees appears, Then with brave resolution they quickly embark,
To cross the high mountains and warn the frontiers.

Brave Harman rode foremost with undaunted courage, Nor left his old
trail these heathen to shun;
His firm resolution was to save Bluestone,
Though he knew by their sign they were near three to one.
The first salutation the Shawnees did give them, They saw the smoke rise
from behind some old logs; Brave Harman to fight them then quickly
dismounted, Saying, "Do you lie there, you save, murdering dogs?"
He says, "My dear sons stand by me with courage, And like heroes fight
on till you die on the ground." Without hesitation they swiftly rushed
forward, They have the honor of taking their hair.
At first by the host of red skins surrounded,
His well pointed gun made them jump behind trees, At last all slain, but
two, and they wounded, Cherokee in the shoulder, and Wolf in the knees.
Great thanks to the Almighty for the strength and the courage, By which
the brave Harmans triumphed over the foe;

Not the women and children then intended to slaughter, But the bloody
invaders themselves are laid low.
May their generation on the frontiers he stationed, To confound and
defeat all their murdering schemes, And put a frustration to every invasion,
And drive the Shawnees from Montgomery's fair streams.

## Part 4

### The Long Journey

### As told by William Neel Harman

Heinrich Adam Harman and his wife Louisa Katrina immigrated to America from Germany with their first born son, Adam, in 1726, along with numerous other Moravian settlers who wanted to escape religious persecution. Along the way, on the Isle of Man, their second son, Henry, was born. The family made their way to the New River area of Virginia and according to a report by surveyors Patton and Buchanan they were the first permanent white settlers in the territory. In 1752 at the age of twenty six, Henry was appointed constable of the New River Area, a captain of "Troops of Horse" and an overseer of the road. He and his family led the way into the wilderness and their attitudes

towards their way of life are exemplified by the final words spoken by his †
mother, Louisa Katrina, as she died on March 18, 1749: "My earthly travels
are over. I fought a good fight. All men must die, and I must leave. Good
night all my loved ones". Henry Harman owned land in Tazewell and other
counties in southwest Virginia as early as 1754. In 1756, he was commissioned
Captain of the King's Militia, a title which stuck with him for the rest of his
life Capt. Harman was also dubbed "Old Skygusty" (Great Warrior) by the
Indians. In 1758 he married Anna (Nancy) Williams and they raised nine
children in the wilderness. Henry Harman was described by a contemporary
as "very tall, of massive frame and very strongly built". In 1787 Captain
Henry Harman, being the senior officer, took command of an expedition to
rescue some captives that the Shawnee had taken in a raid at Burke's Garden.
The Indians were overtaken and Henry planned to attack their camp before
dawn. While preparing to charge the Indian camp, he discovered one of his
staff, Captain Maxwell wearing a white hunting shirt and told him to take it
off because it would be too good a target for the Indians in the dark and the
surprise attack would be jeopardized. The order was not obeyed by Maxwell,
perhaps because he had no other garment to put on. Maxwell was indeed
killed during the first fire; some of the prisoners were killed and scalped, but
two Negroes and Mrs. Ingles survived. The area where this encounter took
place has since been known as Maxwell's Gap.

    The Shawnee frequently raided into western Virginia, crossing the
Ohio River, coming up the Kanawha, New River and Little River valleys
and across the Blue Ridge Mountains. Their purpose was not only to kill the
men and plunder their homes, but to capture women and children to adopt
into their families or to exchange prisoners for ransom back to their families
or during the Revolutionary War, to the British.*In 1760 a large band of
Shawnee invaded the area. Most settlers retreated to their blockhouses and
forts, but some lingered at the risk of life and property. The Indians succeeded
in capturing a Dutch (German) woman, some horses, pots and other items,
and escaped in the direction of Little River. Captain Henry Harman and his
militia was soon on their trail. When the Indians reached a point on Little
River in present day Montgomery County, Virginia, where the ground
was thickly covered with sedge grass, they stopped to rest and cook a meal.
Knowing that most of his militia was raw and undisciplined, Harman placed
Thomas Looney and David Lusk, both tried and true soldiers, in charge of
the rear to rally and bring them into action as the occasion required. Henry,

acting as a vedette, crept forward alone, hoping to surprise the Indians and rescue the prisoners alive. He discovered them behind a large log, eating their meal and laughing and talking with great glee. Pausing not a moment to see where his own men were, or to give a thought to the great danger incurred, he took aim at a tall Indian's back as he stooped to sop his bread and then rose. Harman fired and saw the Indian's back double backward, as a man bends his arm. In an instant the savages sprang behind trees and returned fire. When he left Looney and Lusk, they had told him if the militia faltered, at the first fire of his gun, "They would be at his back". Feeling a hand on his back, he whirled and Looney and Lusk smiled in his face. The shots from the Indian's rifles cut splinters from the tree they were using for cover, sending splinters into their hair and flesh, which weren't picked out until after their return to the fort. At this critical moment, the militia, several hundred yards away, fired their guns and loudly cheered and hurrahed, which so frightened the Indians that they all fled into the sedge grass. Captain Harman leaped over the log and asked the woman in English, how many Indians there were and received no answer; he asked her in German and she answered thirty. He told her to throw herself flat on the ground or the Indians would throw back their tomahawks and kill her. Seeing Thomas Looney watching an Indian approaching a path through the grass, he said "Now Thomas, shoot just like you were shooting an old buck". At the fire of Looney's gun, down went the Indian. The militia came stalking in cautiously and were fired upon from the grass. Two of them fell to the ground: one of whom was killed; the other, known as Little Jack (surname forgotten) had the presence of mind to fall to the ground when the other man was hit and thus he escaped unhurt. The battle continued furiously on both sides, until the Indians, finding seven or eight of their numbers slain, finally gave way on all sides and escaped through the grass, leaving the victorious whites in possession of the field, the rescued prisoner and all the stolen property. Captain Harman returned to the first Indian he had shot and found him sitting with his gun across his lap. Suddenly, moving the muzzle toward his breast, the Indian exclaimed "Wash! Ta!" and fired. He had failed to load enough powder and the ball hung up in the fouled barrel. Harman leaped upon him and dispatched him with his tomahawk. On another occasion, being on horseback and a number of miles from the fort, Henry Harman was waylaid by some Indians and his large bay mare was shot down under him. The mare fell on one of his legs and held him fast to the ground. Seeing the savages rushing upon him with uplifted tomahawks, and being a man of gigantic strength, he drew up the other foot, placed his heel against the mares back and by herculean efforts pushed the huge beast off his leg. Harman leaped to his feet, rifle in hand, and pointing it at their breasts, made them take to the trees for cover. Not giving them time to reload their empty guns, he ran for his life. When they started in pursuit, he again drew his loaded rifle and made them take to the trees, and again ran for his life. He continued to repeat this tactic and gained a little distance from his assailants each time. When he had gained considerable distance, he continued to race without stopping—thinking to outrun them. But while the others lagged behind, there was one fleet warrior, whose speed he could not surpass, who still pressed closely after him. Long and hot was the chase until at length, being so far ahead of the others that he felt sure of being able to dispatch the untiring savage before the others came up, he once more turned and showed him the muzzle of his rifle; at which, the Indian fearing to encounter Henry alone with an empty gun, turned and gave up the chase. The balance of this narrative about the exploits of Henry Harman is reproduced, word for word using the spelling, punctuation and terminology exactly as handwritten by William Neel Harman, grandson of Henry Harman, allowing the true emotions of the participants to be expressed to the reader.

Part 5

Hairbreadth Escapes

Written by John Newton Harman Sr. 1924

Knowing their trails and lurking places, Captain Harman sometimes went alone, as a scout, to discover the approach or whereabouts of the Indians. On one occasion, being on a scout and on foot, he suddenly discovered a large band of them on horseback, coming directly toward him at a point where there seemed no possible way to escape, save by trying to hide himself under some lodged grass beside the path along which they were to pass. Seeing that they had not discovered him he had barely time to throw himself under the lodged and leaning grass. On they quickly came and rode by, Indian file, so close the horses' hoofs almost trod upon him, but passed without seeing him. Thus, he escaped a frightful death and perhaps torture at their hands.

On another occasion, being on horseback and a number of miles away from the fort, he was waylaid by them and his large bay mare shot down under and on him. The mare, falling on one of his legs held him fast on the ground. Seeing the savages rushing on him with uplifted tomahawks, and being a man of gigantic strength, he drew up the other foot, placed his heel against the mare's back and by herculean efforts pushed the huge beast off his leg, leaped to his feet. rifle in hand, and pointing it at their breasts, made them take trees, and. not giving them time to load their empty guns, ran for his life, till. seeing them started in pursuit, he again drew his loaded rifle and made them take trees, and again ran for life, till the pack got started after him, when he again drew his rifle and made them take to trees; in this way gaining a little distance from his assailants every time. Having repeated this operation 'till he had gained considerable distance he now continued to race without stopping-thinking to outrun them. But while others lagged behind, there was one feet warrior whose speed he could not surpass, who still pressed closely after him. Long and hot was the chase, till at length, being so far behind of the others, that he felt sure of being able to dispatch this untiring savage before the others came up. he once more showed him the muzzle of his gun; at which, the Indian fearing to encounter him alone. turned and gave up the chase. and our hero reached the fort in safety.

Part 6

The Battle of Warfield and the Capture of Jane Wily

*Thorpe, West Virginia: The monument for Henry Harman and his sons Matthias and George at the site of the battle of November 12, 1788, with 7 Black Wolf Indians.*

Of all the heroic feats or hand-to-hand death—grapple encounters with the Indians in the border warfare of this or any country -none surpass the superb achievement of Capt. Henry Harman and his sons at The Battle of Warfield on Tug River named in honor of that event. It occurred on the 12th of Nov, 1788. Capt. Harman with his sons George & Mathias (18 years old) and George Draper proceeded with thirty packhorses to Tug River to hunt bears and pack home the meat, and finding a suitable point struck camp-staked out their horses and leaving George (Draper) to prepare their supplies the others went hunting.

Shortly afterwards George discovered what he took to be the signs of Indians and by a signal recalled his comrads from *the hunt. His father examined the signs including a pair of leggings which he smelled and by the smell which he well knew and possessions and their bag recognized the sign to be of Indians-and from appearances supposed to be about 10 in number. A council or consultation was at once held, what was best to be done. There were two ways back to the settlements—one a near & direct route up the river—the other a circuitous mountain route by which it would require several days to reach the settlements. It was known that the men of Bluestone & Abbs Valley were all out hunting—the hunting season having arrived & the women and children left defenseless at their homes and certain prey for the blood thirsty savages. Seeing the Indian trail led directly up the river Draper & the two younger Harmans strongly advocated the mountain route, but the old man whose word was law, with an emphatic gesture declared, "I will warn Bluestone this night at the risk of my life". Noble superb, heroic deed! But for this, the Black Wolf, with his band of Shawnee warriors, now directly in the way up the river route-in no wise appeased by the many massacres & butcheries he had already made in the 11 years preceeding-would have made a perfectly complete holocaust of the women & children of the Bluestone settlements. The line of march was soon taken directly up the river. Draper rode next to Capt. Harman in front and George & Mathias brought up the rear driving the packhorses. At the shake of every bush Draper would exclaim "here they are". Having twice forded the river and directly after ascending the bank from the second crossing a trained bear dog was sent ahead of the men, and that when the dog reared up on a log behind which the Indians were concealed, that he came running back whining, with his hair turned upward down and carrying his tail tucked between his legs. This action by the dog gave the Harmans a moment in which to dismount before the Indians fired upon them.

*Reflections Part I*

Capt. Harman exclaimed "there you lie you sad murdering dogs". They were armed with rifles tomahawks war-clubs, bows and brass-headed arrows. In an instant they rose & fired upon the whites but without effect. But with their terrific war-hoops with which they made the woods resound they now rushed on Capt. Harman with drawn tomahawks expecting in an instant to take his scalp. Draper having at the first fire wheeled his horse and unceremoniously fled. George seeing Drapers flight past him turned his eyes towards his father now half surrounded by his savage assailants and by pointing his loaded gun at them kept them from surrounding him. George heard him call over his shoulder-"good lord, my sons, don't leave me"-George relates that from that moment he knew no fear-rushed to his fathers side and in his eagerness to slay the foremost assailant who proved to be the veritable "Wolf his newly dickert gun used a little too quick but striking & wounding the savage in the knee. The fathers gun—now with deadly aim sent a ball through an Indians heart who fell & expired. The father had taken the precaution to forbid Mathias to shoot & thus kept a loaded gun ready to prevent being tomahawked by the savages—trying to load his gun with his left hand (the Harmans all carried their shot pouches on their left side). George was struck by an arrow which pierced entirely through the double of his arm and with the other hand he jerked out the barb point foremost from behind next to the shoulder & doing so dropped his ramrod. From this wound the blood spouted freely_-being a lame man from white swelling a stout athletic savage seeing him limp and his blood flowing freely deemed him an easy prey.

Throwing down his unloaded gun and advancing on George with up lifted tomahawk, but George by a sudden blow with his gun barrel knocked the top of his head & repeatedly threw the Indian to the ground but the Indian being clad in a tight calico hunting shirt, George found it impossible to hold him long enough to reach his butchers knife which in the scuffle still slipped around his back beyond his grasp. In this life & death struggle so long protracted George at length upon throwing his slippery antagonist got his hand upon his knife and plunged it deep in the Indians side. While continuing to do so over again another Indian took in the situation and advanced on George with a war club which he drew steadily over Georges head to make a sure lick at that moment there was a sharp crack of a rifle. The fathers eye had caught the situation and sent a ball through that Indian. War-club flew high in the air and the Indian with a horsed yell escaping fell prostrate on the ground. It was the fathers rifle. Mathias who had now determined to not shoot but have his loaded gun ever ready, about this time obtained leave and taking good aim killed another Indian. George now beheld Wolf trying to drag off the wounded Indian towards a thicket of laurel on the bank of the river. He drew his rifle, which he had now loaded and made present but the cunning Wolf bounding first to the one side and then the other gained the thicket. While that was going on an Indian Chief calling himself Cherokee (so stated in the sworn narrative of Mrs. Willy) singled out & approached Capt. Harman (whom he called Skigusti-great warrior) for single combat—approaching up close to him, he drew a deadly arrow, and Harman drew his rifle which he had reloaded. Both shot or aimed to shoot at the same moment of time. The cock of the gun lock caught half-cock and it failed to fire. The arrow pierced the double of Capt. Harmans arm cutting a large blood vessel from which as soon as he jerked out the barbed arrow the blood sprouted. Harman again cocked and drew his gun speedily. The savage drawing another arrow advanced till the arrow and the muzzle of the gun passed each other. The gun again missed fire and the arrow struck a rib of Capt. Harman not the heart which glanced around and was finally cutout behind his shoulder. Thinking he had now killed him the Indian jumped behind a sapling as Harman drew his gun for the third time and continued to spring rapidly back & fourth behind the sapling till Harmans gun fired shooting him through the arm near the body—as learned from Mrs. Wily. Soon afterwards Capt. Harman sunk down & fainted from loss of blood. George returning to his side got water & threw in his face & he revived and said we are not whipped, give me my pipe and while he took a smoke George seeing something glitter in the moon light now shining found it was the bright tomahawk of the Indian he had killed and scalped. The Indian which scalp is preserved in the family to this day. The Indians Wolf & Cherokee beholding 4 of their numbers slain and made an escape for life. Wolf shot 1 horse the result made it a cripple for life. The other horse wounded severely of which died that night. The raiders went dragging & supporting their wounded comrade down the warpath where Draper/was hid in a tree-top from which escaping after they had passed. He took his route by the circuitous mountains south to the settlements where the Harmans had already arrived and finding a concourse of people assembled and beginning to tell them that the Harmans were all killed. It is said hearing it George drew his hunting knife and made at Draper and he had to get away from there. The brass & barbed arrow point being cut out behind Capt.

Harmans left shoulder he speedily recovered and lived at his home where we reside now, lived till the fall of the year 1821 with his youngest son (Elias) (the writers father at which date bloody flux breaking out in the family he with other members (of) the family died with flux) about one year from the date of the battle.

In the fall of 1789 a band of Indians led by this same Wolf & Cherokee made another raid into the Bluestone settlements and captured Miss Jane (or Jean) Wily and an infant child of hers._ she being then 9 months of another and carried them down the lower fork of Sandy (River). On the route she became the mother of another child. Whether her husband was killed tradition does not say—no one has noticed or made any record of this event as far as this writer is informed. The property was near the Harman homestead. The Indians carried her to the Harman battleground—Warfield—gathered up the bones of the Indians that died including the one that died the night after the battle, placed them in a hollow log & mourned over them.

Pointing out the exact spot where he fought with Captain Harman. Cherokee said "right there I killed Skigusti", (reckless whether they might kill her Mrs. Wily replied no you didn't for he is now alive & well). He replied you lie, you virginny bitch for when I shot him he called upon his God". They took (her) further down the river and took her and her children into a cave and tied her feet to stakes driven into the ground then they went out for days to hunt. One day they came in hurriedly and said there were some younackys (meaning white men) seized up her two children & knocked their brains out upon the rocks and ran out—leaving her staked to the ground. She now scuffled till she got one hand loose and with it untied the other, and finding herself loose she ran for life toward the river—reaching the bank she hollowed and a man named Adam Harman came to the other bank and hurriedly made a raft of logs, came across and rescued her just as (they) got to the opposite bank they looked back and saw one of the Indians on the bank they had left. She returned to the settlements and went before a Justice of the (Peace) and made oath to the truth of the above narrative. Henry Harman continued to live at the "old Harman house- Holly Brook" in Burkes Garden. After the death of his wife Anna, he continued to live there with his eldest son Ellas. (the writers father) (William Neel Harman) he died in the fall of the year 1827 when together with four other members of his sons family he died being a hundred and one years of age.

NOTE: Henry Harman's grave stone in the Holly Brook Cemetery in Bland County Virginia shows his birth date as 1726 and death as 1822.

## Part 7

### Daniel Harman son of Capt. Henry "Old Skygusty" Harman
### From the annals of Tazewell County, Virginia

Daniel Harman left his house, on the head of Clinch, on a fine morning in the fall of 1791, for the purpose of killing a deer. Where he went for that purpose is not known, but having done so, he started for home, with the deer fastened to the cantle of his saddle.

Harman was a great hunter and owned a choice rifle, remarkable for the beauty of its finish and the superior structure of its triggers, which were, as usual, of the double kind. So strong was the spring of these, that, when sprung, the noise might be heard for a consider. able distance. He was riding a large spirited horse and the lad got within a mile of home, and was passing through a bottom, near the present residence, and on the lands of William O. George, when suddenly a party of Indians sprang from behind a log and fired on him. He was unhurt, and putting spurs to his horse, away he went through the heavy timber, forgetting all other danger, in his precarious situation.

On he went, but his horse, passing too near a tree, struck the rider's knee, breaking his leg and throwing him from his horse. In a few minutes the savages were upon him, and, with their tomahawks, soon put an end to his sufferings. The horse continued his flight 'till he got to the house, at which were several of the neighbors, who immediately went to look after Har-man. Passing near the Indians they heard the click of Harman's well-known trigger. A panic struck the men, and running in zigzag lines, they made a rapid retreat, leaving the Indians to silently retrace their steps from the settlement.

Part 8

Mathias "Tice" Harman
The Founding of Harman's Station

"Mathias Harman was called "Tice" or "Tias" Harman by his companions. He was diminutive in size, in height being but little more than five feet, and his weight never exceeded one hundred and twenty pounds. He had an enormous nose and a thin sharp face. He had an abundance of hair of a yellow tinge, beard of a darker hue, blue eyes which anger made green and glittering, and a bearing bold and fearless. He possessed an iron constitution, and could endure more fatigue and privation than any of his associates. He was a dead shot with the long rifle of his day. The Indians believed him in league with the devil or some other malevolent power because of their numbers he killed, his miraculous escapes, and the bitterness and relentless daring of his warfare against them. He was one of the Long Hunters, as were others of the Harmans, and more than once did his journeys into the wilderness carry him to the Mississippi River. He and the other Harmans able to bear arms were in the Virginia service in the War of the Revolution. He is said to have formed the colony which made the first settlement in Ab's Valley. He formed the colony which made the first settlement in Eastern Kentucky and erected the blockhouse. He brought in the settlers who rebuilt the blockhouse, and for a number of years he lived in the Blockhouse bottom or its vicinity. In his extreme old age, he returned to Virginia and died there. It is said he lived to be ninety-six, but I have not the date or place of his death." —written by WILLIAM ELSEY CONNELLEY, New York, New York Torch Press 1910

From Eagle Oak and Other Poems,
by Captain Samuel H. Newbery.

Come, turn your eyes toward the East,
If you'd enjoy a muse's feast;
Follow yon mountain's line of blue
'Till High Rock's brow shall greet your view
Who lifts his head above the vale
Where sleeps the hero of my tale,
Whose gallant sons beside him stood
In the mountainous solitude;
Their story brief. though coming late,
In simple verse I will relate.

Skyduskee, with his daring sons,
With horses packed, and rifle guns;
George Draper, too, who went along,
Must be remembered in my song.
In search of game, one autumn day,
They took their journey far away—
Perhaps a hundred miles or so,
To where Tug River's waters flow.
The beechen mast was coming down,
And bears were plenty all around.

So, when they reached their camping ground,
The sons were sent to search around
To see if any "Injun Sign"
Might be found along the line
Where they proposed their camp to make,
To roast or fry their venison steak;
If favored luck should grant their aim

And help them to their fancied game,
That each pack horse might have a load
  To bear o'er hills without a road.

Skyduskee's sons, in searching around,
Soon found some Red Men's camping ground
  Where they had spent the night before,
  And cooked and ate their meagre store;
  The burning brands were scarcely cold,
    Their present danger plainly told;
Then, hurrying back to camp, they found
  Their horses hoppled all around,
  Who to their father made report,
  With all the facts to give support.

Skyduskee was a woodsman born,
In danger reared—all fear to scorn,
  Nor reckless in life's battle-field,
  But prudent to no foeman yield
The vantage ground when life's the stake,
  If duty bid precaution take:
  As life was not a useless gift,
Though Red Men claimed the right to lift
  The scalp from any human head
  Even before the scalped was dead.

Soon the horses were all repacked,
To make for home before attacked;
  No time to parley, or to wait—
  'Twas action then, and not debate
  Their safety was in quick retreat,
  But in good order and complete;
  The older ones in front appear,
The Harman sons to be in the rear.
The silent march was then begun—
Each hunter with his loaded gun.

*Kenny Harmon*

While every eye was wide awake,
As looking for some poison snake,
The sullen Indian in his wrath
Was crouched along his narrow path.
Six in number, behind a log,
Out of the sight of man or dog;
Two had bows and arrows strong—
Four had rifles near five feet long;
Had they but known their weapons, worth
They'd wiped the Harmans from the earth.

When at the signal of their chief
The awful silence found relief;
Four rifle balls went whizzing out
And followed close by savage shout.
Bad luck to them—their aim had missed—
Four bullets through the air had hissed.
The Harmans, formed in hollow square,
But Draper was no longer there—
His horse had bore him far away,
Out of reach of the bloody fray.

Skyduskee and his oldest son
Each to his shoulder found his gun,
And, quick as thought—with truest aim—
Indians two were limping lame;
Their combs were cut by Harman's gaffs
That made them squirm and devil's laugh;
The others, then, in maddened strife,
With tomahawks and scalping knife
Around the three were closing in
To put an end to all the din.

But soon they found a loaded gun
Was leveled by the youngest son,
Who, at his father's wise request,
Had kept it to his bosom pressed

## Reflections Part I

With seeming aim, he watched the fray,
And kept the savages at bay;
While father and the older son
Were sending death from smoking gun,
And he above with watchful eye,
Could hear the deathly missiles, fly.

The time for him to act was near;
He saw the chieftain's form appear;
So, anxious he, to try his luck,
As well to test his nerve and pluck,
Permission asked from father near,
Who gave it with a hearty cheer.
On wings of death a bullet flew,
That pierced the Shawnee chieftain through,
Who fell beneath a tall beech tree,
With daring spirit—forever free.

The older son, to tell the truth,
He had been lame from early youth;
His foeman saw him limping 'round,
Mistook his lameness for a wound,
And rushing on him for his scalp—
As well might he attack the Alps.
Though George was lame, he found him tough,
And wiry too—as well as rough—
A rough and tumble fight begun,
Without the aid of any gun.

George Harman's knife was in his belt,
Although for it he'd often felt;
With ease, he threw the Red Man down,
But could not hold him on the ground,
His shot pouch on his left side hung,
In his tussle to his back was clung.
In vain he sought his truant knife,

To put an end to the Red Man's life,
Though failing oft, the time came 'round,
And found him dead on the battle ground.

'Twas hand to hand—and tilt for tilt,
Until the Red Man's blood was spilt.
Whose scalping knife had turned that day,
And to his heart had carved its way;
Whose ghost went out where the knife went in,
Stained with the blood of a brother's sin.
'Twas life for life, the price that's paid
By all who join in be horrid trade—
Savage, civilized—one and all—
The strongest rise, the weakest fall.

Mathias and George had done good work;
None but Draper had seemed to shirk;
Four out of six were put to rest.
The other two, their father pressed
With arrows flying from the bow.
'Till blood began to freely flow.
Whose nerve and pluck was of the best,
One arrow fastened in his breast.
Who seeing that their chief was dead,
Became disheartened, turned and fled.
As through the forest on they sped.
Perhaps not mindful of their dead.

Though twice their number lost or killed;
Their beating hearts forever stilled;
Without a scalp on either belt,
Their woeful luck they keenly felt.
But keener was George Draper's sight,
Who saw them in their onward flight.
All but Draper their duty did;
He, in a fallen tree top hid.
The old tree top he did disgrace
By making it his hiding place.

## Reflections Part I

The battle o'er, the day was won,
By Henry and his worthy sons,
Though two to one had been the odds—
The brave are aided by the gods.
With willing hand, and willing heart.
Half the battle is in the start.
The aim of justice is the right,
Though not always in the fight;
But courage is the god of will
Whose purpose is to rule or kill.

The time to fight had passed away—
To dress the wounded in the fray,
To get the arrow from the breast
Of their father, was then the test.
The bearded arrow head was flared—
And bleeding bosom must be bared
To get the horrid weapon out,
Though followed by a bloody spout.
With pocket knife they cut it loose,
Then worked away the gory sluice;

Then bound it up as best they could—
Determined, then, to leave the wood,
And leave the wilds and wilder still
The Red Man with his stubborn will;
With tomahawk and scalping knife.
Who had pledged his sacred life
To save his father's hunting ground.
Where trespassers were often found;
Which pledge he kept with bloody hand
Till driven from his father's land.

The homeward march was soon begun—
Brave Henry with his valiant sons.
Though somewhat damaged in the fight.
But living foes all put to flight:

Full conscious of their duty done
With hunting knife and trusty gun,
Although their horses bore no packs,
But empty all, and going back,
They'd left their home in search of game,
Returning then—with naught but fame.

George Draper had before them sped—
Reported all the Harmans dead;
While he alone, was only left,
To tell the story to the bereft.
But, by and by, the Harmans came—
New laurels added to their name,
The heroes of a battle won,
Where none but Draper ever run:
The Harmans were of warrior clan—
Their sires came from the Isle of Man.

Skyduskee was of massive frame—
The Red Man gave to him his name
Because he was of stately form, B
Both tall and straight—a soldier born,
With darkened brows and flashing eye,
From dangers front would never fly;
Whose motto was: To never yield
Till every foeman quit the field.
Rather than show the feather white,
Would sink his name in endless night.

I've often seen their battle ground
And fancied I could hear the sound
Of whizzing balls and twanging bows
Between the Harmans and their foes;
Or faintly hear the raven's croak
Amid the branches of the oak,
And flying vultures from afar—
The filthy scavengers of war,

*Reflections Part I*

All, it seemed, had heard the groans,
And swiftly came to pick the bones.

Near six score years have rolled away
   Since that fearful autumn day;
   An Indian, and hunting knife.
   With rifle gun, and date of strife.
Were carved upon the bole of beech,
As high as carving hand could reach.

That noted beech no more appears,
   Although it stood a hundred years
   As monument to mark the place
Where Draper did his name disgrace.
   The sacrilegious hand of man
Has marred the spot, where savage clan
   Once dared to lift his feeble hand
   In the defence of native land;
   With erring judgment, staking all,
   And saw his sylvan empire fall.

# Chapter 2

## Across the Miles

One of the best things about growing up in the '60s is that none of our activities were caught on camera and shared around the world. In 1966, when we wanted to capture moments on film, we had cameras like the Hawkeye, the Motormatic, and the Retina Reflex.

Soon came America's iconic Fotomats. They popped up in parking lots across the country. They started in California, and within two years they spread across to all 50 states. The drive thru kiosk, with the iconic yellow-shingled roof, printed out rolls of film in 24 hours. Today when we take photographs, it takes seconds to appear on our phones and can be shared with the rest of the world in minutes. We forget just how fast these photos can spread, especially when they are poking fun at others or tugging on our heartstrings. In those same 24 hours, that it once took Fotomat to develop a roll of film with 24 photos; we can now share a single photo around the world. That is exactly what happened to Kelsey Harmon on March 16th, 2016 when she snapped a picture of her Papaw at a cookout. The two shared a plate of burgers and home fries that was initially intended as a family meal that included her brother and four cousins. Due to a string of miscommunications, the intended "family barbecue" did not work out as planned. Kelsey noticed that her Papaw was slightly disappointed. She decided to taunt the others with a photo of Papaw taking a bite from his burger. She posted the image to Twitter with the caption: "dinner with papaw tonight…he made 12 burgers for all 6 grandkids and I'm the only one who showed. love him."

The simple snapshot posted to Twitter set off a firestorm of sympathy that nearly broke the internet. In the first 48 hours, the tweet gained over 225,000 likes and 137,000 retweets. By morning, America's beloved Papaw had hundreds of new grandchildren. Media across the country set their sights on Oklahoma and the Harmon family! The online magazine, When in Manila (located in the Philippines) wrote a feature story all about Sad Papaw and his bad burger moment. The website has approximately 10 million views a day.

Media Reactions to Kelsey Harmon's photo that sent Twitter into a meltdown:

*You'll find everything on Twitter: trolls, funny memes, serious news and even heart-tugging photos of sad "papaws." After the tweet went viral, some people harassed the other five grandkids who didn't show up.* - New York Daily News

*Kelsey explained the tweet was live for roughly two hours before it took off, though she says it went viral for the wrong reasons. "I feel like people took it the wrong way or thought it was super sad like no one loved my Papaw or like all my cousins skipped out on him, but that's not what happened at all. We just had dinner and they had other obligations so they couldn't make it."* - USA Today

*Some Twitter users said it made them miss their grandparents. Others turned the photo of "papaw" into a meme.* - wkyc3 (NBC-affiliated television station licensed in Cleveland, Ohio)

*Kenneth Harmon became an internet sensation thanks to a heartrending snap of him eating burgers with one of his granddaughters — Hundreds of thousands of people reacted to Twitter user Kelsey Harmon's photo of her grandfather.* - News 24 (South African Online News Publication)

*Shades of JD & DJ wrote: 'Please tell him that more than 15k people wants to eat hamburgers with him. Big hugs for you two [sic]'. Another user, tweeting under the name Noor Loves Zayn, wrote: 'Now he has 45.9K new grandchildren who would love to have a burger with him I'm in tears this made me so sad I'm crying'.* - The Daily Mail (United Kingdom)

*Some Twitter users said it made them miss their grandparents. Others turned the photo of*
*"papaw" into a meme.* - Entertainment Channel in Australia

*The takeaway message? When grandparents invite you for dinner, show up - to be a good person and to avoid the wrath of the internet.* - Stuff.co.nz (New Zealand News Site)

*For those who are lucky enough to still have their grandparents in their lives, take a moment and call them or have a meal with them. As Kelsey wrote on Twitter, "people need to appreciate their family" because you never know how much time you have left with your loved ones.* - a plus (A Chicken Soup for the Soul Company)

Some of the news affiliates that also picked up Sad Papaw's story include Good Morning
America, ABC News, CBS News, Fox News, the Loop (a social lifestyle website in Canada),
KHQ-TV (channel 6 news station in Spokane, Washington), WZZM (news station in Grand Rapids, Michigan), and WRIC – TV (news station in Richmond, Virginia). Others include New York Magazine, Buzz Feed, and Huffington Post.

The world wanted to come together to support Oklahoma's Sad Papaw, and Kenny gave them that opportunity by hosting a second cookout and this time everyone was invited! The event to take place on March 26th turned out to be bigger than anyone expected. Kenny predicted that there would be 150 – 200 visitors at the barbecue. Brock was paying a little more attention to the responses and advised him that there may be close to 2,000 guests that day.

There were more surprises in store for Kenny on his big day. Johnsonville, makers of the most popular sausage in America, reached out to the Internet sensation and donated approximately 750 burger patties and brats for his upcoming cookout. You may wonder what would make such an influential company in the meat industry want to reach out to this smalltown man. Well, it goes down to one word – Family!

Kenny's picnic was a celebration to honor family, particularly grandparents, that are often forgotten about until it is too late. He wanted to recognize

## Reflections Part I

grandparents across the country and just how important it is to keep in touch. With family being the theme for the day it caught the eye of Johnsonville because they too have been family-focused since their start in 1945. That was when Ralph and Alice Stayer opened a butcher shop, named after the small town that they called home – Johnsonville, Wisconsin. Their sausage was made from a family recipe going back to Ralph's ancestors in the 1800s in Austria. Now here it was, 100 years later, being recognized in America as the "sausage with a big taste."

Almost 20 years after the Stayer family opened the doors to their butcher shop, their Johnsonville sausage was sold daily across the state of Wisconsin. Today the sausage is sold in all 50 states and 45 countries. So, when it comes to family barbecues, the day is not complete without Johnsonville on your plate. The company steeped in family connections cares so much for people that even those that work for the meat giants are not referred to as "employees" but instead are called, "members." And now, in Dibble, Oklahoma, the Harmon family and the Stayer family walked into history together to honor the greatest part of the family – grandparents.

The Hefty company was the next to reach out to Kenny. Their products are a staple to parties and picnics of all sizes. On the day he received his surprise package from Hefty the company sent out this tweet.

When the day of the cookout arrived, it was a picture-perfect afternoon. Mother Nature kept away the rain and compassion for the sad grandfather in the meme brought supporters out in droves. The picnic started at 10:00, and Kenny was stationed at the grill to cook his scrumptious burgers. In time, the line for a Papaw burger was a whopping 40 yards long! Kenny was flipping burgers when his son, Ryan, approached him and volunteered to take over the grilling. That way, Kenny could meet people in the crowd that showed up to show their support. He then spent 6 hours shaking hands and sharing stories with visitors that drove in from around the country.

Mashable.com stated that some people waited in line for 45 minutes to have a photo taken with the famous Papaw. Justin Smith, one of Kenny's supporters, posted on his Twitter account, "Here in Purcell Oklahoma all the way from Virginia to get a burger from Papaw." There were people from Australia, Canada, Germany, and Hong Kong who were vacationing here in America when the Sad Papaw story broke the internet. Each of them decided to drop what they were doing and join Sad Papaw at his barbecue. And one-by-one they drove to the small Oklahoma town to meet the beloved Sad Papaw and enjoy his now-famous burgers. Kenny and his family received visitors from 28 states including Texas, Oregon, Indiana,

Missouri, Nevada, Arkansas, Pennsylvania, Minnesota, Colorado, California, New Hampshire, Illinois, Washington, New York, Florida, North Carolina, Maryland, Mississippi, Louisiana, Arizona, South Dakota, Kansas, Iowa, Michigan, Georgia, South Carolina, Virginia, and Ohio.

Brock Harmon later stated, "The most special moment of the day was seeing my grandpa cry.

A couple of people telling their stories that made him tear up. He was really touched." One of the guests at the picnic was Krysta Levy, a PR specialist for Allegiant Air. She presented Kenny with a set of luggage, "Allegiant Air" memorabilia, and a vacation package for Kenny and 12 family members to travel to Destin, Florida. Allegiant Air had recently announced that they were now making regular, non-stop flights to Destin from several locations, including Oklahoma City. They wanted the Harmons to be one of the first families to have that experience.

Stephanie Pilecki, the Allegiant PR specialist who handles the Destin area, teamed alongside ResortQuest and Emerald Coast Convention and Visitors Bureau to make the vacation a picture-perfect dream for the family. ResortQuest made accommodations for the Harmons to stay at a three-story, condo with 27 adult capacities, in the Dunes of Destin. This was a surprise that no one saw coming.

The barbecue lasted six hours. It was a great day for all who made new friends and reflected on the importance of family. They shared burgers, cold glasses of soda pop, and stories of their own home life. Soon the day came to an end, and the last few visitors drove off. Kenny was then able to reflect on the abundance of support that shown to him from people who arrived as strangers and left as friends.

For the last weekend in June 2016, Kenny and 19 family & friends arrived in Destin, a beach community in Florida, that runs along the Gulf of Mexico. It is the most visited city on the Emerald Coast. They receive 4.5 million visitors every year. Kenny and his family were getting their first experience at what makes Destin a vacation hot spot for so many. The pure white sand that looks like sugar is made from ground quartz crystal from the Appalachian Mountains. It is carried to the Destin shore by way of the Apalachicola River.

While the Harmons were enjoying their visit, Chef Christopher Holbrook, from Signature

Catering 30A, joined the family for another cookout. This time they would do the cooking for Kenny. "He shouldn't have to cook – he's on vacay," said Sarah Bailey, a spokesperson for ResortQuest. This was the first time Kenny had such a large family vacation!

Days after the cookout, Kenny received a gift from Nathalie Kremling. She sent a package of candy and heartwarming note all the way from Leutenbach, Germany. It included a box of Raffaello, a coconut treats, and a box of Toffifee, a caramel cup with a hazelnut in the center, topped in chocolate. Kenny enjoyed the coconut candy the most. He stated, "I've never liked coconut until I ate Raffaellos. I couldn't believe how delicious they are!" Nestled inside the care package, Nathalie included this sweet note:

*Oklahoma City's News 9 Captured this image of the long line of Sad Papaw's supporters.*

*The line for a burger seemed endless, but everyone waiting had great conversations together, making the time go by fast.*

*Jake FM 93.3, from Newcastle, Oklahoma's country music station KJKE-FM, broadcast LIVE from Sad Papaw's picnic.*

*Reflections Part I*

*Kate Nelsen and her friends, Dan Schwartz, and Ryan Gottfried drove from Maplewood, Minnesota to have a burger with Sad Papaw.*

*Sad Papaw with his family and friends proudly showing their gift from Allegiant Air.*

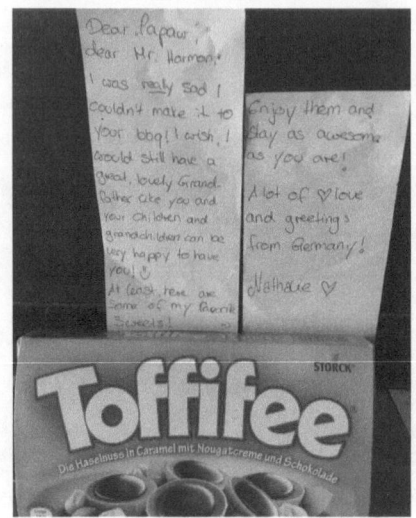

*A lovely note that accompanied the package of candy.*

*Thank you, Nathalie Kremling!*

*Dear Papaw*
*dear Mr. Harmon,*

*I was <u>really</u> sad I couldn't make it to your bbq. I wish I could still have a great, lovely grandfather like you and your children and grandchildren can be very happy to have you. At least here are some of my favorite sweets. Enjoy them and stay as awesome as you are! A lot of♥ love and greetings from Germany!*

*Nathalie♥*

In the weeks that followed the picnic, people continued to show their support and compassion for Sad Papaw from across the miles. One of those people was Yoko, from Japan. She sent him a postcard showing her love and support.

*Kenny being interviewed on ABC 3 WEAR-TV while he was on vacation in Destin.*

*Christopher Holbrook and Signature Catering preparing a feast for the Harmons.*

*Kenny Harmon and his grandson, Brock Harmon, preparing burgers cooked by Chef Christopher Holbrook*

    The barbecue on March 26th was more than a picnic to him. This was a new chapter in his life. Kenny Harmon was once a farm boy who moved on into the world of ironworkers. For years he risked his life every day at work to provide a good home for his family. He was now living a quiet life of retirement. But life was about to reawaken the country boy.

## Reflections Part I

Kelsey and Kenny enjoying the beach in Destin!

Kenny posing with representatives of the condo he stayed at in Destin.

Kenny with Rentie, Manager of the Back Porch Seafood & Oyster House, in Destin.

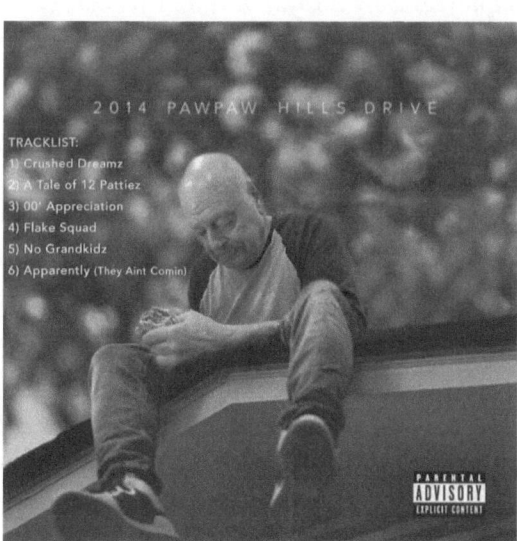

## *Did you know?*

- *Fotomat was one of the first companies to offer movies for rent on videocassette, a new concept back in 1979. Customers would browse through a small catalog, call a number and order the movie of their choice. The following day, the customer could pick up the cassette at the Fotomat kiosk of their choice along with their photos. The rental cost was $12 per title (the equivalent of nearly $40 today), and the customer could keep it for five days. The price later reduced to $9.95 for a five-day rental.*

- *Female employees wore a royal blue and yellow smock top and were called "Fotomates." Male employees were known as "Fotomacs" and wore a light blue polo shirt.*

- *Destin is also known for holding the state's biggest fleet of fishing vessels in its harbor and is called "The World's Luckiest Fishing Village." Every October Destin holds a Fishing Rodeo and a Seafood Festival.*

- *The first magazine was printed in Germany in 1663.*

- *Snickers bars are the most popular candy sold in Oklahoma. Franklin Mars invented the candy bar in 1930. They first sold for a nickel. He always named his candy after things, and this candy bar was named after his favorite horse. (By the way, the name of his ranch was the Milky Way.)*

*The 1962 movie poster for the Maris/Mantle film, "Safe at Home."*

# Chapter 3

# Part 1 A Timeline of Sport's History

From the day that baseball was introduced in America, the Harmon family has been playing the game. Kenny Harmon was a high school athlete and enjoyed playing baseball and basketball. Though he did enjoy football, his school did not have a football team until two years after he graduated. He was lucky to see some of the sport's greatest changes and achievements. For Kenny, the '50s and '60s were some of the most important days in both baseball and football history.

## Part 2

## Baseball Days

We can agree that baseball is the great American pastime but where most people disagree is with WHO created the game? Who is the father of baseball? The Major League Baseball (MLB) organization, which formed in Cincinnati, Ohio in 1869 credits Abner Doubleday with inventing baseball.

The concept of baseball had been around for many years, but it was not until the 1800's that it became the modern sport that we know it to be. The group that gets the main credit for that is the Knickerbocker Baseball Club, named after a New York City fire department. The group was officially formed on September 23, 1845, by Duncan Curry (President), William Wheaton (Vice President), Daniel "Doc" Adams (Secretary), Henry Anthony (Treasurer), William Tucker, and Alexander Cartwright. Each one of them contributed to shaping the rules of baseball. Wheaton, Tucker, and Anderson created the "three outs per inning" rule. Adams had several contributions. He oversaw the creation of the baseball (making many of them himself) and the bat. Adams created the position of shortstop and required the game to last nine innings. He also determined the distance between the bases and the distance from the pitcher to home base. Alexander Cartwright designed the baseball diamond.

On June 19, 1846, with these new rules in hand, the Knickerbocker Club played against the newly established New York Nine baseball team in Hoboken, New Jersey. The New York Nine won the game, 23-1, in four innings. It is considered the first official baseball game because it was played using the Twenty Rules of baseball.

*THE KNICKERBOCKERS TWENTY RULES OF BASEBALL:*

*Members must strictly observe the time agreed upon for exercise, and be punctual in their attendance.*

*When assembled for exercise, the President, or in his absence the Vice-President, shall appoint an Umpire, who shall keep the game in a book proved for that purpose, and note all violations of the By-Laws and Rules during the time of exercise.*

*The presiding officer shall designate two members as Captains, who shall retire and make the match to be played, observing at the same time that the players put opposite to each other should be as nearly equal as possible; the choice of sides to be then tossed for and the first in hand to be decided in like manner.*

*The base shall be from "home" to second base, forty-two paces; from first to third base, forty-two paces, equidistant.*

*No stump match shall be played on a regular day of exercises.*

*If there should not be a sufficient number of members of the Club present at the time agreed upon to commence exercise, gentlemen not members may be chosen in to make up the match, which shall not be broken up to take in members that may afterwards appear; but in all cases, members shall have the preference, when present, at the making of the match.*

*If members appear after the game is commenced, they may be chosen in if mutually agreed upon.*

*The game to consist of twenty-one counts, or aces; but at the conclusion an equal number of hands must be played.*

*The ball must be pitched, not thrown, for the bat.*

*A ball knocked out of the field, or outside the range of the first and third base, is foul.*

*Three balls being struck at and missed and the last one caught, is a hand-out; if not caught is considered fair, and the striker bound to run.*

*If a ball be struck, or tipped, and caught, either flying or on the first bound, it is a hand out.*

*A player running the bases shall be out, if the ball is in the hands of an adversary on the base, or the runner is touched with it before he makes his base; it being understood, however, that in no instance is a ball to be thrown at him.*

*A player running who shall prevent an adversary from catching or getting the ball before making his base, is a hand out.*

*Three hands out, all out.*

*Players must take their strike in regular turn.*

*All disputes and differences relative to the game, to be decided by the Umpire, from which there is no appeal.*

*No ace or base can be made on a foul strike.*

*A runner cannot be put out in making one base, when a balk is made on the pitcher.*

*But one base allowed when a ball bounds out of the field when struck.*

In 1869, Harry Wright, a Cricket player, went on to organize the first professional baseball team, the Cincinnati Red Stockings. There were nine players on the team. They each signed a contract and were paid $950 a year. They played their first game on March 15, 1869, against Antioch College. The Red Stockings won, 41-7.

Babe Ruth may have been a powerhouse on the field, but there was one pitcher that truly frustrated him, possibly out of embarrassment. And that pitcher was Jackie Mitchell. Mitchell only faced Babe once, and he was struck out. The reason it aggravated him is that Mitchell was a 17-year-old girl. She not only struck out Babe, but she also struck out Lou Gehrig right after that. After those two men were struck out, Mitchell faced Tony Lazzeri. Could she strike out all three men – almost. She walked Lazzeri and was then pulled from the game. They said that Ruth was so mad after he struck out that he had them inspect the ball that she was using. Having Mitchell pitch that day was a publicity stunt. They often did things like that in baseball at that time. Before she came out on the field reporters had her posing, powdering her nose. One even stated, she "has a swell change of pace and swings a mean lipstick." After she struck out two of baseball's greatest players, they were not so smug. She was offered a contract to play, but it was never known which team it was because Baseball Commissioner, Kenesaw Mountain Landis, voided her contract. He stated that baseball was too strenuous for women.

Most people believe that Mitchell was the first woman to play professional baseball. Lizzie Arlington was actually the first to play professionally. She pitched for the Reading Coal Heavers in 1898.

In 1908, Jack Norworth and Albert von Tilzer wrote: "Take Me Out to the Ball Game." Fans enjoyed the song so much it became their "unofficial" anthem. The song played during the 7th inning stretch. The funny thing about the song is that Norworth never attended a baseball game. Tilzer did not make it to a game until the late 1920s.

On July 8, 1889, the Giants played their first game at the ballpark known as Polo Grounds. It was a meadow located below Coogans Bluff in Harlem and was adopted by the Giants to be made into their official ballpark. One of the dark days in baseball history happened at that very spot on August 16, 1920. The Yankees were playing against the Indians that day. The two teams were in the middle of a pennant race. Ray Chapman, was described as a "scrappy shortstop," stepped up to the plate. Yankees Carl Mays was on the pitcher's mound. It was a rainy day, and there was a fog in the air. It did not help that the ball they were using was a dark color. Mays was a "spitball" pitcher who was also a master at a pitch called "the submarine." He could get his hand down so low when he pitched the submarine that he often scraped his knuckles on the ground. This time he used a tight and tight pitch. The ball cracked off of Chapman's skull so hard that the sound echoed through the Polo Grounds. The ball rolled back to Mays who thought that Chapman hit the ball. He picked it up and threw it towards first base. However, Chapman did not budge. He collapsed to the ground. Yankee catcher, Muddy Ruel, caught him so that he would not fall hard. They called for a medic, and after a few minutes, they got Chapman to his feet. He took a few steps off the field but collapsed again.

Chapman was rushed to St. Lawrence Hospital. When he arrived, and the doctors saw that he had a depressed fracture, three inches long, on the left side of his skull, they rushed him into surgery. The injury was more than they expected. After they removed a piece of his skull, they noticed that the ball hit him with such force that it lacerated his brain on both sides from hitting the bone so hard. He never woke up. Chapman died 12 hours after being hit by the ball. He is the only baseball player ever killed from an injury in the game.

Mays was known as a "headhunter" for intentionally hitting players with the ball. Ty Cobb was one of those players. He did not take it well, and it sparked a feud between the two. During one of the games when Mays struck Cobb with a pitch, Cobb threw his bat at him in return. Mays called him a "Yellow Dog," and a fistfight ensued. Cobb retaliated in another game when he hit Mays with the ball when he was running towards first base. Once Mays even hit a fan in the stomach with a fastball for heckling him. Mays also gave his teammates a hard time and would often berate them. But hitting Chapman with the ball and later learning that he died was different – a lot different.

Mays swore that he did not hit Chapman intentionally. His friends described May's demeanor as a "complete breakdown." He felt so horrible about it that he even turned himself into the district attorney immediately. He broke down to the DA and explained that he "threw a sailer that came too close." He went on to say, "It was the most regrettable incident of my career, and I would give anything to undo what has happened." The DA explained to Mays that it was an accident and that he would not be charged.

However, other players had a different reaction to the action. Many were infuriated with Mays because they felt the hit was intentional and they were fed up with him hitting the players. The Detroit Tigers and the Boston Red Sox started a petition to have Mays barred from the game and refused to play in any games that he would be a part of. The American League President, Ban Johnson, was quoted as saying, "It is my honest belief that Mr. Mays never will pitch again." The animosity broke up after a while and Mays returned to the pitcher's mound. He played baseball for nine more years. When he left baseball, he stated, "Nobody ever remembers anything about me except one thing, that a pitch I threw caused a man to die."

There have been several rules put into play for the small white ball, other than the fact that it must be bright white while in use. A major league baseball must be made from two pieces of cowhide attached by 108 stitches of red waxed cotton. The circumference of the ball should be between 9.00 and 9.25 inches and weigh 5.00 and 5.25 ounces.

Before each game, each baseball is rubbed with mud from the Blackburne Baseball Rubbing Mud Company. Even though it is mud, it does not dirty the ball. It removes the gloss and makes the bough a little rougher. They harvest the mud from the New Jersey side of the Delaware River. The mud rubbing tradition started in 1950.

**Baseball fans have taken the game to heart from its early days, and it only grew stronger from there. They celebrated many firsts along the way. Here are just a few:**

\*The Knickerbockers were the first to wear baseball uniforms, in 1849. The uniforms included straw hats. Later, the Cleveland Indians and St Louis Cardinals wore jerseys with numbers on their sleeves. It was to make it possible for fans to differentiate among the players on the field. They tried this for only a few games. In 1929, at the start of the season, the New York Yankees and Cleveland Indians took to the field wearing uniforms with numbers on the back of their jerseys. Unfortunately for the Yankees, a storm moved in, and the game was rained out. It was sunny and clear in Ohio, so the Indians proudly played in their new uniforms becoming remembered as the first team to wear numbers on their jerseys. The number was given to mark their batting order. For example, Babe Ruth wore a #3 because he was always third to bat.

*The first rule book of baseball was published in 1877. Changes have been made to the book each year since its release.

*Roger Connor hit the first grand slam on September 9, 1881. He played for the Troy Trojans. He was called "the Oak" because he was unbendable.

*In 1897, Cap Anson, of the Chicago White Stockings, was the first to earn 3,000 hits, starting the "3,000 Club." In the history of baseball, only 26 more players were able to reach that same level of success.

*Chick Fraser, of the Philadelphia Phillies, pitched the first no-hitter on September 18, 1903, against the Chicago Cubs. The Phillies won the game 10-0.

*The first World Series was played on October 1, 1903, between the Pittsburgh Pirates and the Boston Americans, who later became the Red Sox. Boston won!

The World Series was canceled the next year. The champions for the National League were the New York Giants. For the American League, the champions were the Boston Americans. They were supposed to play against each other but John Brush, the Giants owner, had other plans. He and John McGraw, the Giants manager, did not hold a great deal of respect for the American League and said they were not legitimate. They refused to allow the Giants players to compete against the Boston Americans. They went as far as to declare that the Giants were already the Champions because they were the winners in the "only real baseball league."

*In 1905, Roger Bresnahan was the first player to wear a baseball helmet. It was described as "an inflatable boxing glove." Bresnahan later introduced shin guards and padding for the catcher's mask.

*Pittsburgh built Forbes Field in 1909. The first game played there was on June 30, 1909, against the Chicago Cubs. There were 30,388 fans in attendance. The park was named for General John Forbes, a hero of the French and Indian War. Forbes Field would go down in history as the first baseball stadium built in America. What made it stand out from other baseball fields were the three-tier levels. There were ramps and elevators for people to get to their seats. The scoreboard was a part of the outfield wall. There was a grandstand behind home plate, luxury suites, and dugouts on both sides of the field.

*On August 26, 1939, the doubleheader between Brooklyn Dodgers and Cincinnati Reds was the first baseball game played on television. The Dodgers defeated the Reds, 6-1.

*Don Newcombe, of the Dodgers, was the first winner of the Cy Young award. In 1956, Baseball Commissioner, Ford Frick, started the tradition of gifting the Cy Young Award to the best pitcher in the major league - separate American and National League awards began in 1967. The winner is elected by the members of the Baseball Writers Association of America. Frick started the award to honor Cy Young, who died in 1955 from a heart attack.

*On April 6, 1973, Ron Blomberg, of the New York Yankees stepped up to the batter's box at the league's first Designated Hitter. At the time, it was an experiment to see how it would work in the game. It was a success, and having a designated hitter is now part of every team.

Since the early days of baseball, players have been striking balls into the stands, which is thrilling for fans, if they can catch the ball. It gives them a prized souvenir that many fans dive for at every game. It can also be one of the biggest dangers for fans if they get hit by that ball.

And unfortunately, for Alice Roth, she experienced just that on August 17, 1957. But what happened to her was a little different. On that afternoon, Richie Ashburn, of the Philadelphia Phillies hit a foul ball that struck Roth in the face, breaking her nose. The game stopped while she received medical treatment. A few minutes later, they went back to playing. Again, Ashburn hit a foul ball, striking Roth again as she was being carried out on a stretcher. This time the ball broke her knee. This has not happened to another fan in the history of baseball.

Roth was the wife of Earl Roth, sports editor for the Philadelphia Bulletin and was attending the game with her two grandsons. The Phillies treated them impeccably well. The grandsons received tickets and autographed baseballs and were invited into the clubhouse to meet the players. Roth and Ashburn became friends after that day, and her son became a batboy for the Phillies. Ashburn went on to write with Roth's husband for his sports section at the Philadelphia Bulletin.

Throughout the '50s and '60s, the United States was often at war. There was only one year that the nation seemed to be at rest, and that was 1954. The wars seemed to affect every part of society – even baseball! During the war, if soldiers suspected that someone was an infiltrator, they questioned them on their knowledge of baseball. Based on their answers, they could determine if the American soldiers were legitimate. Hand grenades were made in the shape of a baseball because the military knew that many men grew up playing the game. Baseball players, Babe Ruth, Jackie Robinson, Hank Greenberg, Joe DiMaggio, and Ted Williams are just a few baseball players that served in the military. For some players, like Babe Ruth, serving in the military did not interfere with their baseball career.

On August 26, 1943, Babe Ruth participated in an All-Star Game to help raise money for World War II. He took 17 swings against Hall of Fame pitcher Walter Johnson and hit one home run. The event raised $80,000.00.

During World War II, they debated on canceling all of the baseball games until the war was over. Baseball Commissioner Kenesaw Mountain Landis reached out to President Franklin Roosevelt asking for his opinion. Roosevelt quickly wrote back in what came to be known as the "Green Light Letter." He expressed how the country needed baseball for the "recreation, jobs, and overall distraction from the horrors of war."

Twenty-eight-year-old Jackie Robinson became the first African American to play baseball for the National League. He played first base for the Brooklyn Dodgers, and he started on April 15, 1947. That year, Robinson won the Rookie of the Year, having earned 175 hits, 12 home runs, and 48 runs batted in. Breaking the color barrier was just the first f his accomplishments. After he retired from baseball, he went to work for Chock Full O' Nuts, becoming the first African-American to hold the position of Vice President of a major corporation in America. Then in 1962, he became the first African-American to be inducted into the Baseball Hall of Fame. In 1965, Robinson broadcasted

ABC's, "Major League Baseball Game of the Week." This made him the first African-American sports analyst for TV. Robinson later played himself in the film of his life, "The Jackie Robinson Story." Every year after he retired, the Dodgers wore #42 to honor his legacy.

Three months later, Larry Doby, became the first African-American to play for the American League when he signed up to play for the Cleveland Indians. He was good friends with

Robinson, and the two men helped each other through a difficult time of dealing with racism. Both men received death threats, had to stay in hotels separate from the rest of the team and were blocked from using the clubhouse. When Robinson started to play for the Dodgers, several players began a petition to stop him from joining the team. Fans threw racial slurs, among other items, like a black cat! Yes, a fan once threw a black cat at him and yelled, "Hey, Jackie, here's your cousin!"

His teammates also rejected Doby. On his first day of practice, none of them would work with him. That was until Joe Gorgon stepped up and offered to pinch-hit with him. The Philadelphia Athletics were so angry about having to play the Indians, with Doby now on their team, that they hired someone to sit in the stands and harass him. One of the infielders for the Athletics spit tobacco juice in his face.

As new players were stepping onto the baseball field set to break records and carry their teams through winning games and championships, several legends were playing their final games as their careers ended and retirement laid ahead for them. One of the legends lost was baseball pioneer, Babe Ruth. He died on August 16, 1948. Cancer ravaged his body. It started with a tumor behind his nose that caused a stabbing pain behind his left eye. As the tumor grew, it reached the back of his skull. He made his last appearance on the baseball field on June 13, 1948. They were celebrating to mark the 15th anniversary of the opening of Yankee stadium. They played their first game at the stadium on April 18, 1923.

Two teams dominated baseball during the '50s. They were the New York Yankees and the Brooklyn Dodgers. Between 1950-1959, in the National League, the Dodgers won 5 pennants and were World Series champions in 1955 and 1959. In 1955, they won as the Brooklyn Dodgers. In 1959 they won as the Los Angeles Dodgers. During that time, inside the American League, the Yankees won 8 Pennants and 6 World Series championship games –

1950, 1951, 1952, 1953, 1956, and 1958. That was more than any other team. During the 1956 World Series, Yankees pitcher, Don Larsen, became the first pitcher to throw a perfect game in the World Series.

One of the greatest players to wear the Yankees uniform was Joe DiMaggio. DiMaggio's father was a fisherman and wanted his sons to follow after him. But Joe had other ideas. He dropped out of school when he was 16-years-old so he could pursue a career in baseball. While he played in the minors for the San Francisco Seals, he held down odd jobs including working at an orange juice factory and stacking boxes at a warehouse. Twenty-one-year-old, Joe DiMaggio, achieved success on May 3, 1936, when he made his debut with the New York Yankees. He became a phenomenon the day his cleats hit the field. That year he hit 29 home runs. That was the most of any rookie player at that time. Fans brandished him with the name

"Joltin' Joe." Stadium announcer, Arch McDonald, gave him the nickname, the "Yankee Clipper."

On May 15, 1941, DiMaggio got a hit off of White Sox pitcher, Eddie Smith. This started a 56-game winning streak that would go down in history. He was quoted saying, "Getting a daily hit became more important to me than eating, drinking or sleeping." It was on July 17th when Cleveland Indians pitchers, Al Smith, and Jim Bagby, brought his streak to an end. When the streak started, the Yankees were five games behind the Indians. At the end of the streak, the Yankees were six games ahead of the Indians.

Unfortunately, if he had just made it to 57 hits, he would have received a $10,000 endorsement to represent Heinz products - "57 hits for their 57 products." To this day no other player in baseball has been able to break this record. Not everyone was let down by his streak coming to an end. He was remembered in song and in writing. Alan Courtney and Ben Horner wrote Joltin' Joe DiMaggio. The Les Brown Orchestra gave life to their song. Lyrics to the song include:

From coast to coast that's all you'll hear
Of Joe the one man show
He's glorified the horsehide sphere
Joltin' Joe DiMaggio

He'll live in baseball's Hall of Fame
He got there blow by blow

Our kids will tell their kids his name
Joltin' Joe DiMaggio

In 1968, he was in Paul Simon's hit song, "Mrs. Robinson." The song asks, "Where have you gone, Joe DiMaggio? Our nation turns its lonely eyes to you." Though it would be flattering to be in a Paul Simon song, DiMaggio was not sure how to take that. He had the opportunity to meet Paul Simon in a restaurant, and he simply asked, "Why you'd say that? I'm here; everyone knows I'm here." Simon explained that "I didn't mean it that way. I meant, where are all these great heroes now?" Now that he knew what the words meant, DiMaggio indeed was flattered.

He was also celebrated in literature. When Ernest Hemingway penned "The Old Man and the Sea," he included DiMaggio when he wrote: "I would like to take the great DiMaggio fishing,' the old man said. 'They say his father was a fisherman. Maybe he was as poor as we are and would understand.'"

In 1943, he led the Yankees to win the World Series. At the end of the season, he left baseball to join the US Army. He served three years during World War II. He returned in 1946. In 1947, he rejoined the Yankees and picked up right where he left off – leading the Yankees to win the World Series.

Shortly after helping lead the Yankees to win the World Series in 1951, DiMaggio retired from baseball on December 11th. Just a few months before on April 17th, the Yankees introduced their newest player – Mickey Mantle. The Yankees also made it to the World Series that year. In the second game against the New York Giants, Willie Mays hit a fly ball that both Mantle and DiMaggio ran to catch it. DiMaggio called out that he had it and Mantle turned to clear the way for him and tripped over an exposed pipe, damaging his knee. As DiMaggio caught the ball, he saw his teammate fall, not getting back up. He ran to console Mantle and stayed by his side while the waited for medics to carry him off the field. This was the first conversation that Mantle and DiMaggio had together. With all of his accomplishments in baseball, he is also famously remembered for his marriage to Marilyn Monroe. When he died, his last words were, "I finally get to see Marilyn."

Mickey Mantle, the best switch-hitter in baseball history, was from Commerce, Oklahoma. He was signed to play with the Yankees before he even graduated from high school. They offered him $140 per game and a $1,500 bonus. He played on the Yankees minor league for two years before being brought to New York for Yankees spring training. In the first year

Mantle played baseball he had a rocky start. After finishing his first season, he was sent to spend a few months in the minors. He came back in full force and helped lead the Yankees to win the pennant in 1952. On April 17, 1953, Mickey Mantle hit a mammoth home run at Griffith Stadium in Washington, DC. The distance the ball traveled was measured. That began the phrase "tape measure home run."

In 1960, Roger Maris was traded from the Kansas City Athletics to the New York Yankees. He was a great humble player. Maris scored 61 home runs, and Mantle scored 54. In his first game, he hit a single, a double, and two home runs. Halfway through the first season, Maris was injured sliding into second base, causing him to miss 17 games. He still ended the season leading the league in RBI's (112). He was second in home runs. He had 39, which was one behind Mickey Mantle. He also won the Golden Glove Award and was named the American League's MVP.

Both Maris and Mantle were such a force on the baseball diamond that the media dubbed them "the M&M boys." He and Mickey Mantle set the home run record for teammates in 1961. When the season started, they were in a race to beat Babe Ruth's home run record, which was 60 in a single season. In September, Mantle suffered an injury at the hands of his doctor. Long-time Yankee announcer, Mel Allen, recommended a doctor to Mantle when he needed a flu shot. Unfortunately, the doctor injected the needle into his hip bone. It caused him to miss the rest of the season. He was at 54 home runs. Mantle encouraged Maris to continue in his pursuit, telling him, "I want you to break the record!"

On September 26$^{th}$, Maris tied Ruth at 60 home runs. On October 1$^{st}$, the final day of the season, Maris hit home run number 61! Along with baseball achievements. Maris and Mantle had even more in common. They were both sons of miners and were recruited to play football for the University of Oklahoma. The duo also starred together in the 1962 film, Safe at Home. The reign of the M&M Boys came to an end in 1966 when Roger Maris was traded to the St. Louis Cardinals.

Seventeen years after his start in baseball, Mantle retired from the game on September 28, 1968. In that time, he held numerous records, some of which still stand today. Mantle won the Rawlings Gold Glove Award and was one of the few players to win the Triple Crown – meaning he led the lead in three categories in the same season. He played in 16 All-Star games and won the American League MVP three times. He continues to hold the

World Series Records for the most home runs (18), RBI's (40), extra-base hits (26), runs (42), walks (43), and total bases (123).

The Yankees were not the only team during the '50s and '60s to produce some of baseball's most legendary players. There were many more that would one day grace the walls of the Baseball Hall of Fame. A few of those players were Ted Williams, Sandy Koufax, Stan Musial, Bob Gibson, Warren Spahn, Ed Mathews, Roberto Clemente, Bill Mazeroski, and Yogi Berra.

Ted Williams had a batting average of .406 in 1941, and no other player has been able to beat that record. His career average was .344. He missed five years of baseball when he served in World War II and the Korean War. In the Korean War, he learned to fly planes, and his wingman was astronaut, John Glenn. Some of his nicknames were the Kid, Teddy Baseball, and the Splendid Splinter.

Bill Mazeroski, of the Pittsburgh Pirates, went down in history on October 13, 1960. He hit a walk-off home run in the 9th inning of game 7, making the Pirates World Series Champions! The Pittsburgh Pirates played in the first professional baseball game on April 15, 1876. They were known as the Pittsburgh Alleghenies.

Sandy Koufax, of the Los Angeles Dodgers, won the Cy Young Award in 1963, 1965, and 1966. On September 9, 1965, he pitched a perfect game against the Chicago Cubs, which started a record-earning streak. That season Koufax struck out 382 players. It was a record he would hold eight years. Koufax was also the first pitcher to throw four no-hitters. Next to his love of baseball, his spirituality, family, and fans were of utmost importance. When the Dodgers went to the World Series in 1965, he refused to pitch in Game One because it fell on the first day of Yom Kippur. Koufax was also a smoker but would not let photos be taken of him smoking cigarettes because he did not want to be a negative influence on children. Stan Musial, of the St, Louis Cardinals, was born in Donora, a small town in Pennsylvania. Though he was a Pittsburgh area native and cheered on the Pirates when he was growing up, they would not sign him on because they felt he was too skinny. They were impressed with his game, but his weight was a problem for them. He joined the Cardinals in 1941 and stayed with them until 1963. He was a hitting machine that goes unrecognized by many fans. But the Cardinals knew they had a gem. He would become known as the best pitcher ever to play for the Cardinals. Like Koufax, Musial tried to be a positive influence on children.

At the start of his career, he appeared in cigarette advertisements. When he learned about the dangers of cigarettes, he quit smoking and stopped all of the ads.

Warren Spahn, started his career on April 19, 1942, playing for the Boston Braves. In 1957, he went on to play for the Milwaukee Braves. He 1963, he was traded once more to play for the San Francisco Giants. He was a left-handed pitcher who was called the "winningest pitcher" in history. He pitched in 363 winning games, more than any left-handed pitcher. In 1958, he also hit 35 home runs and still holds the National League record for home runs by a pitcher. Like other players, Spahn served in World War II, where he fought at the Battle of the Bulge and earned the Bronze Star, a Purple Heart, a battlefield commission, and a Presidential citation.

Ed Mathews debuted for the Braves on April 15, 1952. He stayed with the team while they were a part of Boston, Milwaukee, and then Atlanta. In 1967, he went on to play for the Houston Astros. A year later he was traded to the Detroit Tigers. For nine seasons in a row, he hit at least 30 home runs, earning recognition as one of the best third basemen in baseball history. In 1957, he hit the game-winning home run, making the Braves the World Series Champions. Legendary Tigers player, Ty Cobb, once described Mathews by saying, "I've only known three or four perfect swings in my time. This lad has one of them." Sports Illustrated magazine debuted on dated August 16, 1954, and featured Ed Mathews, batting for the Milwaukee Braves.

Another significant change in baseball came on May 28, 1957, when the National League approved requests to move the New York Giants to San Francisco and the Brooklyn Dodgers to Los Angeles.

As the 1960s came to a head, the New York Mets would bring the 1969 baseball season to such an amazing end they would go down in history known as the Miracle Mets! At the start of the season, they had never won a World Series, and at one time they were one of the worst teams. In the last three games of the 1969 World Series, it was the New York Mets vs. the Baltimore Orioles. It was the Orioles that were the favorite to win. Few people had faith in the Mets. The Orioles had won the series in 1966, and in the 1969 season, they won 109 games.

The 1969 World Series was all about the Mets. It did not start that way, and not many people had faith in the team. An exciting aspect of the Miracle Mets is that Nolan Ryan was part of their pitching line-up. It was his third year in baseball. By the end of his career (24 years after this game) he would be throwing pitches over 100 miles an hour and have 5,714 career strikeouts. This record would never be broken. Though he had a powerful pitching arm, this would be the only time he would be on a winning World Series team. Throughout those years, seven baseball players who were struck out by Ryan had sons who also grew up to be struck out by Ryan.

The '69 World Series started with a victory to the Orioles. It did not phase the "Amazin' Mets." They gave it their all in Game two and came out champions. From there it was all about the Mets, as they won games three and four, making them the World Series Champions! Nolan This team that never finished higher than 9$^{th}$ put every bit of strength and energy as they went up against the flawless Orioles and showed the world never to underestimate their team again. They truly deserved the name "Miracle Mets!"

## Part 3

### What's In a Name?

When New York installed their first trolleys, pedestrians often had to "dodge" out of their way. In the newspapers, reporters referred to them as "dodgers." This is how their baseball team, the Dodgers, earned their name.

The Atlanta Braves team, which originated in Boston, at one time were called the Beaneaters after the area's famous Boston Baked Beans. In 1912, the name changed to the Braves. From 1936-1941, the Atlanta Braves was known as the Atlanta Bees.

The Pittsburgh Alleghenies were renamed the Pittsburgh Pirates in 1890 when they were accused of "pirating" Louis Bierbauer away from the Philadelphia Athletics.

When the Kansas City Blues relocated to Washington DC in 1901, they changed their name to the Washington Senators. They underwent another name change to the Washington Nationals in 1905. They decided to go back to the Nationals in 1959. The name changed one more (and final) time to the Minnesota Twins.

The Philadelphia Phillies were initially called the Quakers. New owners tried to change their name to the Blue Jays, in 1943. The fans would not accept it, so the change was never made.

St Louis originally had two teams, the Brown Stockings, and the Red Stockings. After a year both teams disbanded. The Brown Stockings came back in 1882. They were called the Browns for short. In 1899, the team's name changed to the Perfectos. The color of their socks changed to red. When a reporter for the St. Louis Republic asked fans what they thought of the uniform changed, one of the young ladies said, "What a lovely shade of Cardinal." The next season, the team was named the Cardinals.

The Brooklyn Atlantics was founded in 1855. In 1888, six players got married in the same season. The team changed its name to the Bridegrooms. They were nicknamed the Grooms.

The Troy Trojans were once a team in New York. They played from 1879-1882. When they disbanded, several players went on to play for the New York Gothams. The team manager used to call them, "My Giants!" When they relocated to San Francisco in 1957, they changed their name to the Giants.

Other names of baseball teams that we no longer have are Providence Grays, St. Louis Terriers, Seattle Pilots, Newark Peppers, Louisville Colonels, Cleveland Spiders, Chicago Whales, and the Brooklyn Tip-Tops.

*Reflections Part I*

# Captured Moments in Baseball

*The first televised baseball game aired on August 26, 1939.*

*Lou Gehrig and Babe Ruth watch an impressive Jackie Mitchell pitch during warm-ups before the game.*

*Baseball fans standing along Coogan's Bluff to watch the game below at the Polo Grounds.*

*Babe Ruth wore a cabbage leaf under his cap to keep him cool. He changed it every two innings.*

*February 15, 1953: Ted Williams narrowly escaped death during a crash landing of a fighter jet in Korea.*

*Honus Wagner of the Pittsburgh Pirates in 1910. Wagner became best known for having his baseball card pulled from cigarette packs sold by the American Tobacco Company. He did not want to promote cigarettes, especially for children.*

*Yogi Berra of the New York Yankees.*

*A 1961 Topps Mickey Mantle trading card showing his "tape measure" home run on April 17, 1953.*

*April 17, 1953 Mickey Mantle hit the first ever "tape measure" home run at Griffiths Stadium in Washington D.C.*

*New York Yankees Whitey Ford, Roger Maris, John Blanchard, Moose Skowron and Bob Hale in 1961.*

*Ray Chapman was the only baseball player to die from injuries he received playing the game.*

*Bill Mazeroski hit the home run that made the Pittsburgh Pirates World Series Champions in 1960.*

*Jackie Robinson and Larry Doby made baseball history when they broke the color barrier and became the first African-American players in the Major League. Robinson played for the National League and Doby played for American League.*

*The pitchers for the 69' Mets – Tom Seaver, Jerry Koosman, Nolan Ryan, Gary Gentry, and Jim McAndrew.*

Mickey Mantle

Roger Maris

## *The M&M Boys!*

Mickey Mantle, Roger Maris, and William Frawley in a scene from the movie, "Safe at Home." William Frawley is also known as his character Fred Mertz from "I Love Lucy."

The M & M boys with Mrs. Babe Ruth.

## Part 4

## National Football League (NFL) Kicks Off

It is hard to imagine that there was once a time when there was no football in the world. The game is not as old as some people may think. The first American football game was played on November 6, 1869. It was a game between Rutgers and Princeton. The game played a lot different than it looks today and that credit goes to Walter Camp, the father of American football. He played rugby for Yale from 1876-1882 and then moved on to coach the team from 1888-1892. The following year in 1893, he revamped the game by combining the rules and plays of association football (soccer) and rugby to develop American football. Camp added the line of scrimmage, down-and-distance rules, the eleven-man team, the gridiron markings on the field, the modern point system, and the legalization of blocking. Camp became quite protective of the rules and disputed anyone who tried to make additions. He particularly did not want the forward pass added. He was not the only one. Several coaches agreed with him. They believed that implementing the forward pass would make the players weak.

On November 12, 1892, William Heffelfinger was paid $500 to play for the Allegheny Athletic Association, in a game against the Pittsburg Athletic Club. He is considered to be the first professional football player. Before that, incentives offered to players were rewards and jobs.

The oval football came about in 1869 from a series of mishaps when inflating balls for a game. They could not get the balls to hold air, so they played with them half full. They liked the shape of the game and believed they performed better with the oval ball. It was redesigned a few more times over the years. It got its modern form in 1905, the same year the forward pass was added to the game. In 1939, they had their first NFL draft. The "huddle" was established in 1899 by Paul Hubbard. He was a legally deaf football player for Gallaudet University from 1892-1895. It was in 1899 when he went on to become a teacher for the Kansas School for the Deaf. He also organized the school's first football team and served as their coach. It was at that time that he established the huddle. It was so he could hear them better, and they could speak in sign language without the other team watching them. Other teams quickly picked up on the huddle and utilized it during their games, as well.

Football was a rough game to play. There was no padding and no protection for the players. They used to create their own protection. Some taped magazines around their shins and others sewed pillows for "shoulder pads." It was creative but not good enough. In 1905, there were 18 players killed on the football field. President Theodore Roosevelt called the colleges together and urged them to develop equipment that would protect the players on the field. A year later they introduced some of the first paddings for the football uniform. They also eliminated the mass formations that would crush players.

In the early 1900s, football continued to rise in popularity, so several clubs were established to form teams. However, it was difficult for some states to find players. Because of that, they were allowed to recruit players from other states. In Canton, Ohio, the American Profession Football Association (APFA) was established to make sure that everyone was playing by the same rules. In the first year of the APFA, they had 14 teams. They were:

Canton Bulldogs
Cleveland Tigers
Akron Professionals
Dayton Triangles
Rock Island Independents
Rochester Jeffersons
Muncie Flyers
Chicago Cardinals
Decatur Staleys
Chicago Tigers
Buffalo All-Americans
Detroit Heralds
Columbus Panhandlers
Hammond Pros

The first president of the APFA was Jim Thorpe. He was a former player and coach for the Canton Bulldogs. Two years after the start of the APFA, it was renamed the National Football League (NFL). Thorpe was born and raised in the Indian Territory, which later became Prague, Oklahoma. His father was Native American, from the Sauk and Fox tribe. He was also French and Irish. Thorpe grew up on the family farm with his twin brother, Charlie. Their father was a horse breeder and taught Jim to hunt and break

## Reflections Part I

horses. As a teenager, Jim could chase down runaway horses on foot. He was fascinated by horses and used to watch the horses run for hours, he then tried to replicate them.

Before Jim turned 18-years-old, he would lose his family, one at a time. His twin died from pneumonia when he was 8-years-old. His mother died from blood poisoning when he was 14years-old. When Jim was 17-years-old, his father died from hunting injuries that he sustained several years prior.

After his father died, he went to live at the Carlisle Indian Industrial School in Pennsylvania. In 1907, he happened to be walking past the track field while they were practicing the high jump and asked if he could try it. He was short in stature (about 5'8"), and the team thought it ridiculous that he believed he could make the jump. They laughed and said "sure" and to be more sarcastic; they raised the bar to 5'9" the highest level. Jim succeeded on his first try. Jim was quickly swept up in the school's sports teams. He became the star of the track team, the baseball team, the hockey team, the basketball team, and the lacrosse team. The sport Thorpe stood out the most in was football. He played for two years and held the positions of halfback, placekicker, punter, and defender. During those two years, the football team only lost two games.

In 1912, after he graduated from college Thorpe was chosen for the Olympic Team traveling to Stockholm, Sweden. He was competing in the pentathlon, a series of five competitions, and the decathlon, a series of 10 competitions. The morning of the event, Thorpe woke up to see that someone stole his shoes. He sifted through the trash and found a pair of shoes that were close to fitting. They were a little big for him, but that did not hold him back. He put his heart into the competition and won two gold medals. When the King of Sweden was putting the gold around his neck, he declared Thorpe to be the greatest athlete in the world. He returned to New York, a hero! New York even threw a parade in his honor. His victory was short-lived. Someone on the Amateur Athletic Union discovered that in 1909 and 1910, he was paid to play on a semi-professional baseball team. They claimed that taking that money meant he was a professional athlete. That would have ruled him out from competing in the Olympics. He was forced to return his medals. They wiped away the records he set at the games.

After the Olympics, his job in professional sports was pitching for the Canton Bulldogs. They won the championship games in 1916, 1917, and 1919. A year later, in 1920, the Bulldogs switched to playing football and joined the AFPA, electing Thorpe as the first President of their club.

When his career in sports came to an end, Thorpe tried his hand at acting. Most of the roles he was offered were those that displayed Indian stereotypes. Thorpe was the type of man who always seemed to make a change wherever life touched him, and Hollywood would soon learn that much about him. He went on to start the Native American Actors Guild. One of their key goals was to place authentic Native Americans in roles, not European men in brown make-up. He also fought for – and won – health insurance and equal pay for Native American actors and stuntmen.

In the last few years of Thorpe's life, he endured a great deal of hardship. After the acting jobs ran out, he struggled to find work. He was an alcoholic, and that depleted his savings. He had surgery for lip cancer in 1950 and had to receive donations and public funding to cover the costs and medical bills. His personal life also had its heartaches. He was married three times, with the first two ending in divorce. His first child to his first wife died from polio when he was four-years-old. In the last few years of Jim's life, he and his wife, Patricia, traveled the country in a trailer. She was Thorpe's third wife. They both enjoyed traveling, so this lifestyle was a great fit for the two of them. Thorpe often spent time fishing and hunting during stops.

He died from a heart attack on March 28, 1953, when he was 64 years old. That was his third heart attack. Patricia wanted to have Thorpe buried in Oklahoma but only if they would agree to build a monument for him. They refused. She was worried that he would end up in a potter's field, so she decided to auction off his remains instead. However, the towns of Mauch Chunk and East Mauch Chunk, Pennsylvania approached her with another offer. They wanted to merge their towns and name their new community, Jim Thorpe, Pennsylvania. They even wanted to build a mausoleum to hold his remains. She agreed and gave his remains to them. Jim Thorpe, Pennsylvania established in 1954.

There was a movie about Jim Thorpe's life that premiered in 1951. The film "All American" starred Burt Lancaster. Kenny was among the group of his friends to watch it in the theaters. Kenny looked up to Thorpe and his achievements, and Burt Lancaster was his favorite actor.

Red Grange, of the Chicago Bears, was the first football player to become famous among the fans. He was also the football played used in endorsements. In college, Grange played for the University of Illinois. He had such great speed and moved so swiftly that Warren Brown, who wrote for the Chicago

American, gave him the name the Galloping Ghost. The name would follow him into the major leagues.

Grange signed on with the Chicago Bears in 1925. In his first five games with the Bears, he scored three touchdowns. By the end of that same season, Grange ran 401 yards. Because of a dispute with the Bears, he left after the first season. He formed his own team, the New York Yankees, and played halfback for the team. He also worked with businessmen, Charles Pyle, and General Charles Zimmerman to establish their own football league – the American Football League (AFL). There were nine teams which included Grange's New York Yankees, along with the Union Quakers of Philadelphia, Boston Bulldogs, Brooklyn Horsemen, Chicago Bulls, Cleveland Panthers, Los Angeles Wildcats, Newark Bears, and the Rock Island Independents. They hoped to rival the NFL, but the AFL league only lasted a year. Red Grange went back to the Bears in 1929 and stayed with them until 1934. In 1932 he made the final plays that won the Super Bowl for the Bears. Red Grange owned the New York Yankees, a football team from 1926-1928 and also the team's halfback. They were a team from 1946-1949.

There were several attempts to revive the AFL, in 1936 and again in 1940. Both times it only lasted a year. The fourth and most successful version of the AFL version established in 1960. The men who started this AFL group hoped to own NFL teams, but the NFL denied them. This AFL included the Boston Patriots, New York Titans, Buffalo Bills, Houston Oilers, Los Angeles Chargers, Denver Broncos, Oakland Raiders, and the Dallas Texans. The Texans moved to Kansas and became the Kansas City Chiefs. The Titans relocated to New York and then named the New York Jets. This time the AFL would last for ten years.

Football fans have long considered, the 1958 Championship game between the Baltimore Colts and the New York Giants to be the greatest game ever played! The game was played on December 28th at Yankee stadium. This was the first time a championship game went into sudden-death overtime. It would not happen again until 59 years later, in 2017. The moment that clinched the victory for the Colts came when Johnny Unitas handed off the ball to Alan "the Horse" Ameche. The final score: 23-17! Baltimore Receiver Raymond Berry threw 12 receptions in that game. It was a championship record that stood for 55 years. Johnny Unitas was also a record player for the Colts. It was an impressive triumph considering this was only his second year playing professional football. He spent his first year with the Pittsburgh Steelers. Between 1956-1960, Unitas held the record for the most consecutive games with a touchdown pass. This record held for 52 years. His strong plays on the field earned him the name, "the golden arm."

Before Unitas became a legend in the NFL, he played college football for the University of Louisville. His first choice was Notre Dame, but they turned him down because of his small frame. After college, he went on to play for the Steelers. They were also concerned with his size and released him after a year. He then worked in the steel mill and played football on the side for the Bloomfield Rams. They were a definition of a sandlot team. Before each game, they sprinkled the ground with oil or water to keep the dust settled. The Rams paid him $3 a game. A few months later, he was invited to try out for the Baltimore Colts. He knew this was his last chance to make it onto a professional team. He was so financially strapped that he had to borrow gas money to make the trip. He left Baltimore with a contract in his hand that would pay him $7,000 to play for the 1956 season. It was the break that he needed, not just for his football career but for his wife and children, as well. He went on to become one of the greatest players in Colts history.

The AFL and NFL became rivals over the years that followed. This lead to the leagues planning a championship competition. The top team from each league was set to meet on the football field on January 15, 1967, in the first-ever AFL-NFL World Championship Game. Lamar Hunt suggested changing the name to the Super Bowl. He thought of the name during a meeting they had to discuss the upcoming game, and his daughter interrupted with her new toy "a super ball." He thought the name was catchy and put a spin on it to create the name - Super Bowl.

The day arrived, and the two teams entering the field were the Green Bay Packers and the Kansas City Chiefs. The Packers would end the game in a victory of 35-10. There was a halftime show of Al Hirt playing his trumpet, two marching bands and 300 pigeons.

Tickets to the game cost $6-$12 each. The game aired on two television stations, ABC and NBC. At the start of the second half, NBC was still airing commercials, and they missed the Packers kicking off the beginning of the second half. The referees asked the Packers to kick off again. Kenny was one of the lucky people to see the first-ever Super Bowl!

The Packers were such a powerhouse of a team that they would go on to win the second Super Bowl as well. They defeated the Oakland Raiders on

*Reflections Part I*

January 14, 1968. Such excitement would grow through the years to come that the game would go from being aired on two stations to 170 countries.

Since football season starts in one year and ends in the following year, they started putting a Roman numeral to indicate which super bowl was being played instead of the year. Officials thought it would make it less confusing. This tradition began in 1971, with Super Bowl V. Footballs used in Super Bowl games are inspected carefully. Every single football used in every Super Bowl has these words on it: Wilson, Commissioner, and Made in the USA. The Wilson Sporting Goods Company in Ada, Ohio, has made footballs since the NFL started in 1941. They make approximately 2 million footballs a year.

In 1966, the AFL merged with the NFL to become one league. Another change made was the coveted trophy awarded to the winning team of the Super Bowl - the World Championship Game Trophy. In 1970 it was renamed the Vince Lombardi Trophy. Lombardi was the coach of the Packers and led the team to their Super Bowl victories.

## Part 5

### What's In A Name?

The Detroit Lions chose their name to correlate with the city's baseball team– the Tigers.

The San Francisco 49'ers was named for the men who had partaken in the gold rush in 1849.

The owners of the Tampa Bay Buccaneers chose the name from the pirates that often raided Florida coasts in the 17th century.

The Baltimore Ravens were named after Edgar Allen Poe's, "The Raven." The team's first three mascots were even named Edgar, Allen, and Poe.

The Indianapolis Colts began in Baltimore, where there was a history of horse breeding. It was the inspiration for the team to be named the Colts. When the football team relocated to Indiana, in 1984, they kept the Colts name.

The Philadelphia Eagles were initially named the Frankford Yellow Jackets. They were renamed the Eagles in 1933. The team's owners Bert Bell and Lud Wray chose the name from the eagle that was the symbol of the National Recovery Act (a part of Franklin Roosevelt's New Deal).

When Rankin Smith started a football team in Atlanta in 1966, he had a contest to choose a name for the new team. Some of the suggestions were the Peaches, Vibrants, Confederates, Firebirds, and Thrashers. The winning name was the Falcons. A few people suggested the name, but they appointed Julia Elliot as the winner because of the reason she chose the name Falcons. She stated, "The falcon is proud and dignified, with great courage and fight. It never drops its prey. It is deadly and has great sporting tradition."

The Buffalo Bills were originally named the Buffalo Bison. When the team underwent changes, the owner held the contest for a new name. The person who chose the name picked it from Buffalo Bill Cody.

There have been several teams who selected their names from contests. They include the Los Angeles Chargers, Jacksonville Jaguars, Denver Broncos, Miami Dolphins, New England Patriots, New Orleans Saints, Seattle Seahawks, Tennessee Titans, and the Pittsburgh Steelers.

Other names of football teams that we no longer have are Hammond Pros, Frankford Yellow Jackets, Providence Steam Rollers, Staten Island Stapletons, Canton Bulldogs, Rochester Jeffersons, Pottsville Maroons, and the Milwaukee Badgers.

Part 6

Oklahoma Sooners

Before the country had the NFL, Oklahoma had the Sooners – the University of Oklahoma's football team. It was 26 years after football was invented and 12 years before Oklahoma was even a state. There was a time when college football was more popular than even baseball, the great American past time. And in the '50s no one played the game better than the Oklahoma Sooners. In 1949, they had an undefeated season and went on to win the Sugar Bowl in 1950. They defeated Louisiana State University (LSU), 35-0. A few days before the game, LSU's offensive lineman, Walter "Piggy" Barnes, was caught spying on the Sooners during their practices. Oklahoma's coach, Bud Wilkinson, caught him in the act with a telescope and a camera in his hands. When he approached him, Barnes ran off with Wilkinson running close behind him. Barnes ran to the home of a former LSU teammate and refused to come out when coach Wilkinson knocked on the door. From 1947 to 1963, the Sooners won six of eight bowl games and compiled a winning percentage of .826.

This victory was just the beginning of a winning decade for the Sooners. In 1954, they won the Orange Bowl, defeating the Maryland Terrapins, 7-0. Don't let the low score fool you, it was an exciting game, and the teams ran 500 yards. Going into the game, the Sooners were the underdogs.

Two years later, they were on the field again – Sooners vs. Terrapins. The Sooners were not just trying to win another Orange Bowl championship; they were also maintaining a 30game winning streak! By the end of the first half of the game, Terrapin was winning 6-0. Well, the half-time break gave Oklahoma the second wind they needed. They roared back onto that field winning their second Orange Bowl Championship of the decade, 20-6.

In 1958, the Sooners were back in the championship games trying to secure another victory! They were playing the Duke Blue Devils, and both teams were playing their hearts out. At the start of the third quarter, the Sooners were winning, 21-14. The Sooners steamrolled over Duke at the end of the game, achieving an additional 21 points – with the game 48-21!

The Sooners closed out the decade, the same way they brought it in – as Champions!! That's right! In 1959, the Oklahoma Sooners were Orange Bowl Champions again, defeating Syracuse Orangemen, 21-6! It was the 25$^{th}$ anniversary of the Orange Bowl, and the Sooners made it amazing! OU Daily described just how fascinating each play came about for the Sooners. The first touchdown came from a 42-yard rush. Brewster Hobby achieved the second touchdown as he completed a halfback pass to Ross Coyle, who took it 79 yards for the score. Hobby was instrumental in the third touchdown as well. It was delivered from a 40yard punt return from Hobby. Oklahoma Sooners became the only college football team to win four championship games in one decade. From 1947 to 1963, the Sooners won six of eight bowl games and compiled a winning percentage of .826.

*In the 1956 Orange Bowl the #1 ranked Oklahoma Sooners beat the Maryland Terrapins 20 to 6.*

*A rare photo of an emotional Coach Wilkinson.*

*Bud Wilkinson recruited the smartest players, then taught them readiness, discipline, and character.*

*Reflections Part I*

*Jim Thorpe preparing for the Olympics.*

*Jim Thorpe when he played for the Rock Island Independents.*

*The Decatur Staleys in a game against the Rock Island Independents (striped shirts).*

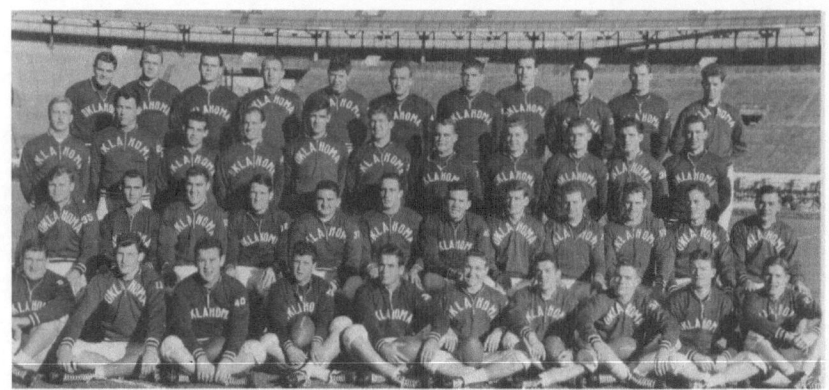

*The Oklahoma Sooners were the Sugar Bowl Champions of 1949.*

*1956 Orange Bowl: Tommy McDonald was the most versatile player during the Bud Wilkinson Dynasty (1947 to 1960).*

*Reflections Part I*

*Billy Vessels running for a touchdown against Notre Dame in 1952. Also that year, Vessels became the first Sooner to win the Heisman Trophy. He was one of the Sooners best players in the 50's.*

*Sooners beating Duke 48-21 in 1958 Orange Bowl.*

*The Oklahoma Sooners defeated Syracuse Orange in 1959 for the Orange Bowl Championship title.*

## *Did you know?*

*In Football...*

- *The Green Bay Packers defeated the Kansas City Chiefs in the first Super Bowl on January 15, 1967. Tickets to the game cost $6.*

- *Fred Haise graduated from Oklahoma University in 1959. He was an astronaut on Apollo 13.*

- *The waiting list o get season tickets to the Green Bay Packers is approximately 955 years.*

- *Deion Sanders is the only person to play in a Super Bowl and a World Series.*

- *More pizza is sold on Super Bowl Sunday than any day of the year. Pizza and chicken wings are the most popular snacks eaten on Super Bowl Sunday. Along with that, Americans consume over 1 billion chicken wings, 8 million pounds of guacamole, 11 million pounds of potato chips, 4 million pounds of pretzels, and 2.5 million pounds of nuts. They also drink 50 million cases of beer. (Sales for antacids rise by 20% the day after the Super Bowl.)*

*In Baseball...*

- *It is a rule that a pitcher must first wipe his hand on his uniform before he grips the ball for a pitch.*

- *In the early days of baseball, the players nicknamed an easy fly ball a "can of corn." It came from when grocers used their aprons to catch cans knocked from a high shelf.*

- *When Jimmy Pearsall hit his 100th home run in 1963, he ran the bases in the correct order but facing backward to celebrate.*

- *Mickey Mantle, Gil McDougald, and Yogi Berra all used the same babysitter for their children. Her name was Martha Helen Kostyra. She later became known to the world as Martha Stewart.*

- *To keep cool, Babe Ruth used to keep a cabbage leaf under his cap. He would throw it out and use a new leaf after every two innings.*

*Reflections Part I*

*In the early 60's Dibble School Principal, Warner Hayhurst told his wife, Olga, (Kenny Harmons' third grade teacher), that when he filled one of his boots with coins he would buy a new car. In 1963, Mr. & Mrs. Hayhurst went to Knippelmier Chevrolet and bought that new car. In this photo, Mr. Hayhurst is on the left and Mr. Knippelmier is on the right. Inside the car, Mrs. Hayhurst is in the drivers seat and Mrs. Knippelmier is sitting in the passenger seat.*

*The Studebaker Offices in 1852.*
*At this time they were repairing covered wagons.*

77

# Chapter 4

# Part 1 Kenny, Cars... and Cruisin'

The '50s gave birth to the Ford Thunderbird, the Plymouth Fury, and the Chevy Corvette. The Blanchard community was dotted with several car dealers. One of those was Jack Ramsey Dodge, who changed to selling Chevys in 1949. The original owners were Jack Roddy Jr, Fred Wilkerson, and Homer Trout. In 1959, Trout bought out Wilkerson. There was also Knippelmier Chevrolet. For 30 years, it was owned and operated by Ray & Inis Knippelmier and Larry & Peggy Knippelmier.

On Wednesday, January 12, 1966, Kenny turned 16-years-old. There was one big thing he was looking forward to the most - getting his driver's license! Kenny already knew how to drive from working on the farm. One of the first vehicles he drove was Babe's '50 Chevy and the De Soto owned by Nellie's brother-in-law, Dewey Merchant. However, getting his license was his ticket to being able to go cruising with his friends, taking dates to the drive-in, and going to parties! And of course, he can do more errands for his parents, but let's face it, picking up dates was at the top of the list.

In 1899 the New York Times coined the word "automobile." Two terms commonly used by car buyers in the '50s and '60s were "sports car" and "muscle car." Though the models have a lot in common, there are some differences in the engine, body, and torque. Due to their smaller size, sports cars are easier to handle, especially making driving around bends. With muscle cars, enthusiasts can make additions for fun and convenience. Unfortunately, muscle cars are more expensive due to the size of their engines.

## Reflections Part I

Automakers have competed on a design for the fastest car since 1890, a few short years after Karl Benz built the first automobile. Henry Ford stated said, "Auto racing began 5 minutes after the second car was built." As for who made the first sports car, well, that dispute has never been settled. Since carmakers cannot agree on the exact specifications that a vehicle needs to receive the moniker of "sports car," it is hard to tell which car can be given the title of "first sports car." We do know that a sports car is defined as a low, small, usually 2passenger automobile designed for quick response, easy maneuverability, and high-speed driving. The '50s gave birth to the modern sports car, and the Nash-Healey was the first of that decade. Other popular sports cars of the '50s include the Ford Mustang, Buick LeSabre, Porsche Spyder, Jaguar, Ferrari, Corvette, Camaro, and the Mercedes-Benz 300SL. Another sports car was the Corvette. It was made in 1953. It was not as successful as they thought it would be, and they almost did not make one in 1954.

Other cars to make their debut in the '50s include the Station Wagon (1957), the VW Beetle, and the VW Microbus, which was nicknamed the "hippie van." Many people believe the Microbus to be the first minivan, but the 1935 Stout Scarab was the first "minivan." Only 6 Stout Scarabs were made. Enthusiasts can see the vehicle at the Owl's Head Transportation Museum.

There were several significant features added to cars in the '50s. Power steering and the hardtop convertible was introduced in 1951. Power Braking was first used in 1952. The typical car had four drum brakes. In 1954 GM introduced the Autotronic-Eye which would automatically dim the high beams when a car would approach and then turn them back up when the oncoming car passed. Cruise control was added to vehicles in 1957. In 1959, the Ford Galaxie was introduced and cost $3,233. It was one of the favorites among the cars that year because the engine was described as a beast!

The '60s was the Golden Age of muscle cars, and Blanchard had a few choices car lots that Kenny remembers fondly. There was Jack Ramsey Dodge that opened in 1946 and was initially owned by Jack Roddy Jr., Fred Wilkerson, and Homer Trout. In 1959, Trout bought out Wilkerson.

The Oldsmobile Rocket 88 was introduced a year earlier, in 1949. CarsDirect noted that some recognize the Rocket as the first muscle car. Still, others believe the first muscle car was the 1964 Pontiac GTO. (By the way, GTO stands for Gran Turismo Omologato.) Other types of muscle cars include the Chevy Bel Air, the Hudson Hornet, Dodge Charger, Shelby Mustang, Oldsmobile Toronado, the Boss 429, Chevelle, Fairlane, Plymouth

Road Runner, the SuperBee, and the Pontiac Catalina. The American Motors Corporation had the Big Bad AMX Pack. It gave car buyers the option to purchase their bumpers in either orange, green, or blue. In 1968, Dodge called their muscle cars the Scat Pack. Plymouth referred to their muscle cars as the Rapid Transit System.

In 1960, the Ford Falcon was new to the automobile world, and the name behind the car has an interesting story. Edsel Ford first created the name Falcon for a car that he was designing, but he later felt the name just didn't fit and changed his design to the Mercury. General Motors decided they wanted the name but had to register the name before their rival – the Ford Motor Company. They did not succeed! In fact, Ford only beat GM to the registration office by 20 minutes.

Henry Ford II unveiled the Mustang at the World's Fair in Flushing Meadows, New York on April 17, 1964. The car sold for $2,368. There were 22,000 Mustangs sold on the day. Before the Ford Mustang was named, they toyed with other names such as Avventura, Torina, Cougar, Comet, and the Allegro. Gale Halderman designed the Mustang and was hoping that they would name the car the Cougar. The phrase "pony car" was coined by drivers because of the horse-name of the car. Phil Clark designed the Mustang that was showcased on the car's grille. Some of the cars show the Mustang galloping from right to left, but the Ford company decided to keep the Mustang galloping left-to-right, the way Clark designed it. Some believe it was drawn this way because he was left-handed. Chevrolet, wanting to keep up with their competitor, introduced the Chevy Camaro a year later.

The very first Mustang, nicknamed "Wimbledon White," was on a dealership-tour and on one of its stops it was accidentally sold to Canadian Eastern Airlines Pilot, Stanley Tucker. The Ford company was desperate to get back the car that was emblazoned with the identifying mark of "serial number one." It took some coaxing, but they were able to repurchase the car, which included a brand new Mustang in the exchange. The Mustang he was given was the one-millionth Mustang made by the Ford company. The Wimbledon White is now on display at the Henry Ford Museum.

The Mustang Maniac group described how in October 1965, Ford engineers sliced a 1966 Mustang into four sections and took it up on a passenger elevator to the 86th-floor observation deck of New York's Empire State Building, where it was reassembled and placed on display.

## Part 2

## Little Bit of History

In 1860, Ettiene Lenoir built the first internal combustion engine, which started the domino effect of mankind's attempt to find a quicker and more convenient form of transportation. Nikolaus Otto improved on his engine in 1876. Many of today's engines are still built from his design.

On December 31, 1870, BF Goodrich, started adding carbon pigments, used by Binney & Smith to make crayons, to make the white tires - black. He found that the pigments made the tires stronger and more durable.

In 1899, a 68-year-old man, named, Henry Bliss, was helping a friend from a streetcar when taxi driver, Jacob German struck him. Bliss became the first person killed in an automobile accident, and German was the first person arrested for speeding.

In 1901, New York made a law that automobile owners had to put their initials on their cars. They used metal letters on leather pads which cost $1. That was the introduction of the license plate. It became law for vehicles to be registered in 1908. Stop signs were first used in 1914. The traffic light was first used in Detroit in 1919.

Rims for tires were made in 1906. Since then, each decade introduced new additions to the automobile to make it quicker, more reliable, safer, and convenient. Additions include:

In 1901 speedometers were added to automobiles.

Glass windshields and windshield wipers were made in 1903.

The rearview mirror was made in 1911.

Car heaters were added in 1917.

The four-wheel brake and the back-up light were added in 1923.

In 1926 the semi-automatic car was made.

The first automobile with a convertible top was made in 1927.

Cars were first wired for radio in 1929, though the radio was sold separately.

They added air conditioning to cars in 1933.

In 1937 the gear shift was moved from the floor to the steering column.

The 1940s brought sealed headlights and tubeless tires.

Carmakers introduced power seats in the '40s.

Mercury and Ford were the first to use power windows. It was in their Sportsman convertibles in 1946.

It was in 1950 when seat belts were added to vehicles.

Part 3

Making Drag Racing History

Henry Ford was quoted as saying, "Motor racing started after the second car was built." There are no truer words than that. The first time a car traveled down the rocky roads, carmakers were already thinking of ways to make it better – and faster! Through the years, car engines were made with more power and were eventually able to reach speeds of up to 100 miles an hour, thus giving birth to the "speed demons."

The next phase of this crowning achievement was organized racing. The sport of racing that started with horse races in Kentucky would soon include Formula Racing, Stock Car Racing, and Off-Road Racing. For Kenny and his friends, Drag outshined them all. No one is certain how it got its name, but many believe that it is because the first races took place in small California towns through the streets or the 'main drag,' earning the name drag racing. These races grew in popularity. It was much to the dismay of many California residents who frowned upon these races taking place through their neighborhoods. There were three types of competitions.

*Reflections Part I*

1. Chicken: It included two opposing cars that would accelerate toward each other to see who would scare first and either slam on the brakes or swerve and bring their car to a stop.

2. Crinkle-Fender: This is where cars would repeatedly wreck into each other until one quit or their car stalled.

3. Pedestrian Poker: Drivers would see how close they could get to a pedestrian without hitting them.

It was in the 1930s when drag racing moved from the streets to the dry lake beds and abandoned military airstrips in California.

Oklahoma native, Wally Parks organized the Southern California Timing Association (SCTA) in 1937. They are a competition governing body of 11 car clubs whose job it is to maintain the rules and records for Land Speed Racing held at El Mirage Dry Lake, California and the Bonneville Salt Flats, Utah. When they first established, they comprised of only five car clubs. They first met on November 29, 1937. Their goal that day was to create an official set of rules for drag racing along the dry lake beds, to make the sport safer. Those rules became the foundation of racing rules for future organizations. The rules included safety regulations, axle ratios, make, model, year, and engine specifications. The SCTA remains the oldest running racing organization in the United States of America.

Wally Parks was a World War II veteran who was born in Goltry, Oklahoma. His family moved to California when he was in middle school. His first job in the automobile industry was as a military tank test-driver for General Motors. In 1951, Parks founded the National Hot Rod Association (NHRA) to help further regulate the safety of the sport. As he put it, he wanted to "create order from chaos." It was the NHRA that helped Drag Racing earn its spot as an official sport. One of their achievements was to classify drag races into two sections: 'Unmodified Stock' and 'Top Eliminator.' In 1958, they started keeping a record for elapsed time (E.T.) and Speed records. It was Drag Racer Bobby Wood who broke the first record.

In 1950, CJ Hart, along with Creighton Hunter, built the first official drag strip on an unused runway at the Orange County Airport. It became known as the Santa Ana Drag Strip. It was meant to be a safer place, than the streets, for adrenaline junkies to race their hopped-up cars. It was a place to let their bad behavior spill out in a way that would no longer be a danger to the residents of the streets where they once raced. The races were held on Sundays and cost 50 cents to either participate or watch the race. Approximately 50 cars would participate in the races. Hunter sold his part of the business to Hart a year after they opened. Hart's wife, Peggy, took over as his partner. She often competed in the races in her '33 Willy's Coupe. She even won several times. The Santa Ana Drag Strip closed in 1959 when the airport expanded and needed the use of the runway back.

Don Garlits, "the Father of Drag Racing," became the first professional drag racer in 1955. He was a skilled engineer and built his first race car in the front yard of his home in Florida. It was a 1927 Ford Model T Roadster. He added to it a 1948 Mercury engine block, a 1939 Ford floor shift transmission, and a 1948 Ford differential and axle. The car could reach 93 miles an hour in 13 seconds. It was also the car he was driving when he won the first NHRA race that he entered, the NHRA Safety Safari. When Garlits moved from Florida to California in 1959, he was given the nicknames, "the Floridian" and the "Swamp Rat." He did not mind that name, and after that day, each car he created was branded with the name "Swamp Rat." He became the first driver to wear a Nomex race suit, with the hopes of encouraging other drivers to do the same; and they did. Unfortunately, the next mark he would make in drag racing history came at a cost. In 1970, while racing his car, the Swamp rat XIII, the transmission exploded. This caused the vehicle to split in two and cut off his right foot. This tragedy did not scare Garlits away from racing. He explained, "That's when I drew up plans for what I thought would be a championship rear-engine car. I would go out to the shop in Seffner on my wheelchair, saw stuff out on the band saw and make the parts." The result was a race car with the engine in the rear of the vehicle, away from the driver. Two years later, this became the template to be used when designing race cars.

Dragster, Eddie Hill, was the first to attach a parachute on the back of his car to assist in braking. He made this adjustment in 1959 and soon after it became mandatory for cars that reached over 150 mph. Hill won his first race in 1947 when he was only 11-years-old. He was 19-years-old when he entered and won his first drag race. His hot rod had a Model T frame and an Oldsmobile V8 engine. It would be the first of many victories to come. As a drag racer, he earned the nicknames, "the Thrill," "Holeshot Hill," and "Fast Eddie." After racing cars, he moved on to racing motorcycles and then boats. After suffering from broken bones in a boat drag race, he went back to racing cars. Upon returning, the car he used in the first race had the engine from that boat wreck. He was able to retrieve it from the bottom of the lake. Throughout his career, he won close to 200 trophies.

The NHRA held its first-ever Championship Drag Races in Great Bend, Kansas, on September 1955. One of the drivers that day was Art Chrisman. His top speed in the race was 145 mph. That was a record for a single-engine car that would remain unbroken. His father, Everet, brother Lloyd, and Uncle Jack were all drag racing drivers. Art often drove cars designed by his Uncle Jack. His achievements in racing were recognized in several ways. He earned a spot on the NHRA's list of Top 50 Drivers of All Time. He was awarded the Robert E. Petersen Lifetime Achievement Award and was inducted in both the SEMA's Hall of Fame and the Motorsports Hall of Fame.

The NHRA hosted its first Winternationals event at the Los Angeles County Fairgrounds in 1961. The race is sometimes called the "Winternats." Chrisman won that race! In 1963, Peggy Hart (wife of Pappy Hart) fought for the right of Carol Cox to race in the Winternationals. Not only did she become the first woman allowed to participate in the Winternationals – she won! The race track still stands today, and the Winternationals are still growing strong.

Don "Dyno" Nicholson started drag racing in high school. He was indeed an adrenaline junkie, which caused him to accumulate so many speeding tickets he could not possibly pay them all. He agreed to join the Navy in exchange for dismissing all of his tickets. Once out of the Navy, he and his friends held races in modified jalopies. These races did not contain many rules or much structure. Sadly, several of his friends were killed while racing. In 1949, he moved to California to compete on the dry lake beds. Once there, he mostly did the engineering work. He did not go back to racing until 1958. It was then that he earned the name "Dyno" for being the first driver to use a chassis dynamometer. In 1961, he won his first Winternationals. He and fellow race car driver, Ronnie Sox, were the only ones driving Chevrolets in the race that day. The rest were all Fords. He won again in 1962. Throughout his career, he won 90% of his races. According to the NHRA, this record was never broken.

Drag Racer, Shirley Shahan, was one of the first women to Drag Race professionally. Shahan started driving when she was only 10-years-old. As a teen, she worked as her father's mechanic while he was drag racing. Her first drag races were on the streets of California. She often beat the boys in her father's Studebaker pickup that she had developed into a racing dream.

When she entered Drag Racing, her husband worked as a flagman. There were often protests held to keep her, "a woman," from entering races, especially when she entered the NHRA's first March Meet (US Fuel & Gas Championship Race) in 1959. Shahan went on to win that race, in her Super Stock 1958 Chevrolet; making her the first woman to win an NHRA national race. She beat 40 other drivers, including Dyno Nicholson. When Shahan won the Winternationals in 1966, she made the cover of National Dragster magazine. Shahan competed in Drag Racing until she was 70 years old.

Chris Karamesines got his start in drag racing in 1959. He became known as the "Golden Greek" and the "Rod Father." That same year, he won his first National Race, the World Series of Drag Racing at Cordova, Illinois. A year later, at the Alton Dragway in Illinois, in his Chizler dragster, he reached speeds of 204.54 mph, making him the first dragster to reach speeds over 200 mph.

Racecar owner, Muncie Dragway, and NHRA board member, Larry Carrier, left the organization in 1970 because of constant feuds with Wally Parks. Many believe that Carrier did not dislike Parks. The animosity between the two men grew because they were so competitive with each other. Carrier was not always easy to get along with though. He was opinionated and stubborn, so much so that he was called the "Rebel of Drag racing." Together, Dragway and Carrier established the International Hot Rod Association (IHRA). While at the IHRA, Carrier was able to sign-on the first major company to sponsor drag racing. They were the RJ Reynolds tobacco company. The first thing Carrier did to celebrate was to take them to meet Parks. That was mostly to rub in his victory.

Carrier's assistant had a unique way of describing Carrier's attitude. *"If anyone wanted to feud and throw mud, Larry was like a big kid with a squirt gun. The minute someone was ready to get it on, he was right there, ready. I think he did it a lot for the publicity because people were still amazed that he dare do something like that. He would come up with little slams and digs. He would know how far he could go without turning people against him. He knew when to stop and when he was close to going over the line."*

In spite of his brash personality, Carrier was sharp as a tack when it came to the business end of drag racing. His group, IHRA still stands and continues to hold a prominent position in the racing field.

Kenny started watching drag racing on TV in the early '60s on ABC 's Wide World of Sports. He attended his first sanctioned drags (the word often used for drag racing) in 1967 at the San Valley Raceway in Oklahoma City. Buck Hall, one of Kenny's lifelong friends and baseball teammates, was sitting next to him at the first drags he attended. The announcer stated over the PA that it was time for the Nitros. Buck hollered, "Kenny if one of those things blows up it'll kill all of us!!" Buck thought "nitro" was nitroglycerin. In fact, "Nitro" was short for "nitromethane," a type of fuel used in the fastest cars and dragsters.

Kenny was a fan of racing that involved Chevrolets! He was also a fan of the stock cars and the rapidly changing category titled, " Funny Cars." In 1963 and 1964, some of the Super Stock teams began experimenting with chassis set-ups, body designs, fuel mixtures, fuel delivery systems, and engines. The first name for these new Super Stocks was called "Bashers." Since there was not a sanctioned category for the Bashers, they only had match races. The name was soon changed to "Match Bashers." People started commenting on how the cars looked funny. From that, the name changed again to "Funny Cars." In 1965, they were inducted into the NHRA as a specific classification of a drag racing vehicle.

Chrysler designed the first Funny Cars, typically made from muscle cars. Their trademark design was a carbon fiber automotive body and the tilt-up fiberglass (made from a single flattened sheet of fiberglass). The "carbon fiber" was an extremely strong sheet of plastic made of carbon fibers. It gave them the appearance of being showroom model cars, but slightly off, earning the name "funny car." The engine of a Funny Car is in front of the driver, instead of the rear. That made it stand out from other cars. Also, the rear tires were larger than the front tires, and they were placed further up the chassis. They were sometimes called "Floppers" because they "flopped along."

Bruce Larson, of Linden New Jersey, was a champion at racing the Funny Cars. Larson started drag racing, at 16-years-old, in 1953. His first car was a fender less 1932 Ford Coupe. He quickly won many local racing competitions which caught the eye of racing fans and the NHRA. He was invited to compete in national competitions and immediately started racking up championship titles. In 1968, he set the National Funny Car elapsed times (E.T.) record of 7.41 seconds.

Larson traveled to York, Pennsylvania in 1969 to participate in the Super Stock Nationals, a race that he won! He celebrated by redesigning the image of his car. He added a license plate that read "USA-1." He painted the car red, white, and blue. He also added stars and the words "USA-1" to the side of his car. That new design became an iconic symbol in Funny Car history.

Throughout his career, just some of the races that Larson won were the Winternationals, Springnationals, Mile-High nationals, Seafair nationals, Fallnationals, and the Winston Finals.

The string of championship wins earned him a spot inside the Don Garlits International Drag Racing Hall of Fame, the East Coast Drag Times Hall of Fame, the Eastern Motorsports Press Association Hall of Fame, the Pennsylvania Sports Hall of Fame, and the Super Stock Magazine Drag Racing Hall of Fame.

James "Jungle Jim" Liberman was one of the top Funny Car drivers to participate in the sport. He was born and raised in West Goshen Township, Pennsylvania. When he was in 11th grade, he dropped out of high school and moved to California to participate in Drag Racing. His second year there he joined the circuit of Funny Car drivers. Liberman was known to be a showman at drag racing events, performing such stunts as driving backward at 100 mph doing his burnout. He once did wheelstands for the full length of the track in a race against Don Nicholson. During his career, he participated in nearly 100 events a year and became known as the "greatest showman the drag strip has ever experienced."

On September 9, 1977, he was back home in Pennsylvania, on the West Chester Pike, when his 1972 Corvette street car collided head-on with a SEPTA transit bus. Liberman was driving at such an excessive speed when they crashed that it took rescue workers 45 minutes to extricate him from the twisted metal.

Altered Races Cars were introduced in 1956. They were race cars with parts removed or alterations that made them ineligible for any other category. That year, in March, the Smokers Car Club hosted their first national championship race, the U.S. Fuel and Gas Championship at Famosco Raceway, in Bakersfield, California. Bob Hanson won that race, with speeds of 136 mph, earning the title of Top Fuel Eliminator (TFE). By the 1960's Altered Race Car drivers included Tim Perry, Dave Benjamin, Jimmy West, Ed Moore, Phil Miller, and Dennis Geisler. The NHRA stopped the Altered Eliminator category races in 1972. The last race for Altered cars was in 1977 at the Winternationals in Pomona, California.

The most famous Altered driver was Wild Willie Borsch. He started racing Altereds in 1960, with his car the Winged Express. On September 28, 1967, at Irwindale, he became the first Altered Driver to break speeds over 200 mph. He won the Winternationals in 1967 and 1968, in the fuel-altered category. He was known for driving with one hand (his right hand), using the other hand to brace himself against the car. When Willie drove asked by Revell Model Makers to drive the Wild Man Dodge Charger, he attached a dummy arm to the side, to symbolize his habit of driving with one arm. Wild Willie was later inducted in the International Drag Racing Hall of Fame. He also earned a spot on the NHRA's list of 50 Greatest Drivers.

Bill "Grumpy" Jenkins was one of Kenny's favorite drivers. Throughout Jenkins's career, he grew famous for his unique and talented work on engines. Jenkins often made modifications to his Chevy engines. He went on to build 30 cars that broke national records.

Most drivers got their start in drag racing by renovating their own cars. A trade they learned when working in repair shops. Jenkins's story is a little different from that. He grew up in Malvern, Pennsylvania and started engineer work fixing his neighbors tractors when he was a teenager. While in high school, he started drag racing in his 55' Chevy Corvette on the streets of Berwyn, Pennsylvania. After he graduated, he went on to Cornell University to study Mechanical Engineering. In his second year of college, he started working for Chevrolet, where they called him "Jiggs." His first job at Chevy was with the dealer, 'Old Reliable' Ammon R. Smith, to modify engines on his race cars. Jenkins gained recognition in the racing field when Strickler's Chevys started setting national E.T. records. He soon went from working on the engines to also driving the cars. It was then, in 1963 that he started a career in drag racing. A year later, he joined the US Drag Racing team and traveled to the United Kingdom to compete in the First International Drag Festival. The National Hot Rod Association selected the team of drivers. The US Team was victorious!

While working for Strickler, Jenkins began driving the Super Stock Bel Airs and Impalas. In 1966, Jenkins started his own racing team with a '66 Chevy Nova named "Grumpy's Toy." It was then that his nickname changed from "Jiggs" to "Grumpy." He earned the nickname "Grumpy" for his "no-nonsense" attitude with racing. Jenkins also became known for using Roman numerals for numbering each of his new Super Stocks and Pro Stocks.

In the 1960's he competed in the A/MP (Modified Production) category. In 1965, he finally won the title at the NHRA Nationals, at the Indianapolis Raceway Park in a 1965 Plymouth Gasser. He had of 11.11 seconds. That same year he won the S/SA class, at the Winternationals, with a pass of 11.39 seconds.

He retired from racing mid-season in 1976. Larry Lombardo and Ken Dondero continued using Grumpy's cars for racing. Retirement did not stop him, though, as he continued his engine work on cars driven by his racing team. He later did engine work for NASCAR. He was featured in Time magazine in 1971. That was the first time drag racing was given recognition in the mainstream media.

Drag Racing started as a way for speed demons to "drag" their souped-up cars to the streets of California for a night of racing fun and simply hanging out with friends to see who would be the first to reach 100 miles an hour. It has since grown to an official sport. It is chock full of racing societies, safety regulations, and international competitions. Cars used in the races can travel up to (and sometimes over) 300 miles per hour. Long live the tradition of racing and the need for speed!

*Reflections Part I*

*Did you know?*

*The driver's license was introduced in 1906.*

*In 1908 headgear for female drivers was introduced.*

*The first Camaro was black and was initially named the Panther.*

*In 1913, the Model T became the first mass-produced car. Three years later, 55% of the cars in the world were Model T's. This achievement has never been matched.*

*The first 30 years of automobiles in Oklahoma, brought on the need for more roads and bridges. So, the Oklahoma Highway Commission was established on March 16, 1911. The group later became the Oklahoma Department of Transportation.*

Don Garlits is the Father of Drag Racing.

Kenny Harmon

*William Harley and Arthur Davidson with the first Harley-Davidson. It was made in 1914 in a 10 by 15-foot wooden shed. It was a bicycle that was converted into a gasoline-powered vehicle. The motorcycle sold for $285.*

*The first sanctioned drag race in Goleta, California. This photo was taken by Eric Rickman and Bob D'Olivo of Petersen Publishing. A company that would go on to print Motor Trend and Hot Rod magazines.*

*James Dean & the car he was driving when he was killed.*

## Reflections Part I

*Bill Jenkins and Larry Lombardo in winners circle with their car "Grumpys Toy."*

*A hemi-powered "altered" Fiat Coupe.*

*The early "Funny Cars" were known as "Match Bashers." The Rambunctious was one of the funny cars raced in 1964.*

*Shirley Shahan was one of the best Super Stock drivers of the '50's and '60's.*

*A flagman getting ready for NHRA's first Championship Drag Races in Great Bend, Kansas.*

*Before John Wayne International airport was established, racers gathered on the abandoned air strip designed by CJ Hart and Creighton Hunter to remove drag racing from the streets of California and onto a race track of their own*

*"Jungle Jim" during a pre-race burnout.*

*In 1969, Liberman took two Chevy Novas to the NHRA Winternational Funny Car event. Clare Sanders (right side of trophy) won the race driving one of his cars.*

*Bill "Grumpy" Jenkins won the "Super Stock" championship at the '67 US Nationals*

## Reflections Part I

"Wild Willie" Borsch was
"King of the Alrereds"

In 1958 Bobby Wood set the first N.H.R.A. record driving his C/Stock Chevy.

Drag Racing Champion Bobby Wood switched to driving Funny Cars in 1965.

The transmission explosion that severed part of the right foot of Don Garlits, March 1970.

*A rare photo of Marilyn Monroe without makeup.*

*1943: 17-year-old Norma Jeane Mortenson before she was known as Marilyn Monroe.*

In 1951, Marilyn Monroe attended a party at the Beverly Hills Hotel wearing a red dress. The "provocative", low cut dress, drew the ire of a female journalist, who called her 'cheap and vulgar'. She even went on to say that Monroe would have looked better wearing a potato sack.

A few days later, Twentieth Century Fox took advantage of the situation and organized a photo shoot that saw Monroe posing in a potato sack dress, that was designed especially for her. The pictures featured in newspapers across the country.

# Chapter 5

# Part 1 Music and Movies that Changed a Generation

The Nifty Fifties and the 60's Generation of Peace and Love brought in a treasure trove of new talent in television, movies, and especially in the music world. The music was more than entertainment. It was chock full of emotion during a time of war, recovery, love, and anger. The music world came a long way from the days of Beethoven.

Movie-goers got their first peek at soon-to-be legends James Dean, Gordon MacRae, Grace Kelly, Jayne Mansfield, and Dorothy Dandridge. Ironically, Macrae's first film was "Oklahoma!" Mansfield had her first role as a cigarette girl in the 1955 film, Pete Kelly's Blues. Dandridge became the first African-American woman to be nominated for an Academy Award.

Tony Curtis and Rock Hudson were also relatively new to the scene. Rock Hudson made his premier in 1948 when he starred in Fighter Squadron. He only had one line, but it took him 38 takes to get it right. Several actors of TV and film called Oklahoma their home. They include TV actor Tony Randall, James Garner, and child actor Ron Howard. Tony Randall was born on February 26, 1920, in Tulsa, Oklahoma, as Aryeh Leonard Rosenberg. Ron Howard was born March 1, 1954, in Duncan, Oklahoma. His family moved away when he was five years old, and he started acting. James Garner was born in Norman, Oklahoma, on April 7, 1928. He played football and basketball for Norman High School. Before he got his big break in Hollywood, Garner served in the Korean War and had a hard time finding steady employment. He went through 75 jobs. He made his film debut in 1956 when he starred in "The Girl He Left Behind." He was later inducted into the Hall of Great Western Performers of the National Cowboy and Western Heritage Museum.

In 1950, children rushed to the theaters to see Cinderella. The film saved the Disney movie franchise. They were 4 million dollars in debt, due to a string of costly flops. Some of the biggest movies of the '50s were the Seventh Seal, Wild Strawberries, The Giant, 12 Angry Men, All About Eve, Rear Window, Vertigo and The Day the Earth Stood Still. One of the favorites for Kenny and his friend was Godzilla, starring Raymond Burr. That opened the door for a successful TV career for Burr, who went on to star in Perry Mason and Ironside. The '60s brought on the future classics The Apartment, Cool Hand Luke, To Kill a Mockingbird, The Haunting, The Wild Bunch, Guess Who's Coming to Dinner, and Easy Rider. Action/thriller films that debuted include The Horror of Dracula, Psycho, The Thing from Another World, Night of the Living Dead, and Rosemary's Baby.

The movie, Psycho, was loosely based on the story of Ed Gein. Three actresses did the voice over for Norman Bates. Alfred Hitchcock mixed their recordings until he got the "voice" just the way he wanted it. Kenny was too afraid to watch Psycho in the theaters. Hitchcock wanted to protect the surprise ending of Psycho. He would not let movie reviewers see it in advance, and there were signs in the lobby telling people that have seen the movie to keep the ending a secret.

The Thing from Another World was one of the popular horror films in 1951. The effects in the movie were so well made that you cannot tell by watching that in the scene where they form a ring around a flying saucer that is frozen in the ice, it was actually 100 degrees outside. James Arness was so embarrassed by his role of the Thing that he did not even go to the film premiere. He said the Thing's costume made him look like a giant carrot.

There were two young men who felt differently than Arness, as they sat on the edge of their seats watching the movie in their own hometowns. One of those children was John Carpenter, who was in such awe of the film that he knew then and there that he wanted to grow up and make movies - and he did. He even played excerpts from it in the first Halloween movie. It was the scene when characters, Laurie Strode (Jamie Lee Curtis), and Tommy Doyle (Brian Andrews) were watching TV on Halloween night. The movie playing on their TV was the Thing from Another World. And it did not stop there for Carpenter. He played homage to his favorite horror film by making a remake 31 years later, titled The Thing.

## Reflections Part I

A few states away, in Illinois, a 9-year-old Roger Ebert was also in the theaters watching The Thing from Another World, a movie that he said: "scared him to death." Ebert also watched Carpenter's remake, The Thing, and he hated it so much that he told people to watch it with a barf bag.

John Wayne also disagreed with the opinion that James Arness had on his portrayal of the Thing. Wayne was offered the leading role on Gunsmoke but turned it down, highly recommending Arness instead, who was then offered the part.

The Seventh Seal also frightened movie-goers in 1957. It was about a man living through the era of the Black Plaque. He has questions about life, death, and the existence of God. To gain the answers to his sought-after questions, he competes against the Grim Reaper in a game of chess.

Kenny started going to the Royal movie theater, in Pauls Valley, in the early '50s. A few years later he began attending the Ritz in Blanchard. He and his friend, Butch Ladd, would also meet up with a group of others from Blanchard at the movies. In October 1955, Kenny and his friends were among the movie theater crowd that went to see Rebel Without a Cause. The movie starred James Dean, who just starred in his first film a few months prior. That film East of Eden, pushed the young James Dean's career, making him a favorite among teens and young adults.

His next big film was "Giant" that co-starred Rock Hudson and Liz Taylor. He was hoping that with "Giant" he would not become typecast as a rebellious teen. Unfortunately, the release of his next film, Giant, was bittersweet because 24-year-old James Dean was killed a few weeks prior in a car accident. Dean was known for his rebellious nature with a fondness for speed and racing. He was actually on his way to compete in the Salinas Road Race when the accident occurred. His mechanic, Rolf Wutherich, was at his side in the passenger seat. Just 2 hours before the accident, Dean received a speeding ticket. He was driving 65 mph in a 55 mph zone. But at the moment of the crash, he was not speeding. The accident was not his fault, at all. The Porsche Spyder he was driving hit a Ford Tudor Sedan that was being driven by 23-year-old Donald Turnupseed. Witnesses claim that Turnupseed drove into the path of Dean's Porsche, to reach the Route 41 Exit. However, Turnupseed explained that the glare from the sun made it impossible to see Dean's car. Turnupseed survived unscathed. Wutherich was severely injured after being thrown from the vehicle, but he too survived. Dean died in the ambulance on their way to Paso Robles War Memorial Hospital.

Before James Dean landed his first acting job, he advertised Pepsi on posters and in commercials.

James Dean filming "Giant." He died before the movie was finished.

When James Garner starred in the Rockford Files he had a special license plate made for the Firebird he used. The first half referred to August 1953, when Garner landed his first acting job. The OKG stood for his home state and last initial.

James Bumgarner (James Garner) (center) played football and basketball for Norman High School in Norman, Oklahoma.

## Reflections Part I

Many people say that James Dean's car (the Little Bastard) was cursed. Fellow actor Alec Guinness (who later played the part of Obi-Wan Kenobi) told him that it was a bad luck car because the serial number was a palindrome: 550-055. He told him if he drove the car, he would be dead in a week. That was seven days before the accident.

After the crash, they were loading the mangled car onto the back of a truck, and it rolled off. It crushed the legs of a mechanic that was standing nearby. They sold parts of the car to a variety of people. Each person that bought a piece from his car was also killed in a car accident.

Before his break in East of Eden, Dean played in a variety of TV shows and as an extra in several movies, including Sailor Beware and Has Anybody Seen My Gal. His first acting job was for a Pepsi Cola commercial. Ironically, a few months before his fatal car accident, James Dean was in a Public Service Announcement about being careful on the highway. He even stated: "Take it easy driving. The life you might save might be mine

For Kenny Harmon, one of his favorite movies was The Curse of Frankenstein. It released on June 25, 1957. It was based on the book, Frankenstein, published in 1818 by Mary Shelley. She wrote the story when she was 18 years old.

The story behind what drove her to write Frankenstein is just as interesting as the book itself. She was on vacation in Switzerland with her husband during a time that they call "a year without a summer." Mount Tambora erupted in Indonesia that caused drastic changes to the weather. Switzerland endured what felt like endless rainstorms. There were several other families on vacation in the same area, and the rain had them stuck inside. They passed the time by reading and sharing ghost stories. Lord Byron then suggested that they hold a writing contest to see who could write the best ghost story. Four people competed, and Mary Shelley won with her story, "Frankenstein." After it was published, the book was known to be the first science fiction novel, and she was credited with creating the image of the "mad scientist." John Wayne was a favorite with fans of Westerns, and it was when he starred in Rio Bravo in 1959 that he became a recognized "cowboy" around the world. The British Film Institute proclaims that it is one of the best films ever made. In 1960, he starred in the Alamo, a film that hit him personally. He was so dedicated to seeing the film hit the movie theaters that he mortgaged his home, his apartment in New York, his automobiles, and even his production company, Batjac Productions. He worked with financial backers to build a replica of the

Alamo on a Bracketville Ranch. That project alone cost 1.5 million dollars. He had to forgo his profits and work another film for free to pay for the costs to make the film. It continued to make the list of best movies ever made, but John Wayne did not make one cent. His wife, Pilar Pallete, remembers how hard he worked and stated that by the end of production he was smoking three packs of cigarettes a day and lost 30 pounds. Pallete said, "He wasn't making a movie. He was on a crusade."

After he starred in True Grit, in 1969, he finally won his first Oscar. An iconic scene that would stay a favorite of western movie fans was a shoot-out scene on horseback, with John Wayne brandishing a pistol in one hand, a rifle in the other and the horse's reins in his teeth. John Wayne's start in Hollywood began in a way that he was not even expecting. After all, most actors grew up with a dream to star in the movies – but not John Wayne. He was a football player at the University of Southern California (USC) with a major in Pre-Law. He suffered a broken collarbone in a bodysurfing accident and was no longer able to play football. Because of that, he lost his football scholarship. The next thing to go wrong for him was that he could not afford to pay his room and board at the fraternity, so he dropped out of school altogether. His former football coach, Howard Jones, helped him get a job as a Prop Guy at Fox Studios. The studio did this as a favor for Jones. They felt they owed him for giving western film star, Tom Mix, free tickets to USC games.

While he was working in props, he used to listen to stories of the old west by the Studio's consultant. That man was Wyatt Earp. His stories fueled John Wayne's desire to work in film, particularly 'westerns.' Wayne credited Earp with helping him develop his "walk, talk, and persona." Three years later he made his debut when he starred in Big Trail.

And yes, John Wayne, whose real name was Marion Morrison, was picked on when he was growing up for having a "girl's name." In high school, he gave himself the nickname "Duke," which he stole from his favorite dog. Fox Studios also had a problem with his feminine name and decided to make a new one for him. The head of Fox Studios was a fan of Revolutionary War General Anthony Wayne, so he honored his hero by giving Morrison the last name of "Wayne." They tried a few different names, for his first name, before they decided that 'John' sounded best. And "John Wayne" was born and ready to show off. Wayne developed lung cancer in 1964. He tried to lessen the fears of the Studio Heads and coined the phrase, "the Big C." Though he was able to beat lung cancer, 15 years later he developed stomach cancer. That time he would lose his battle with the Big C. He died a few months later on June 11, 1979.

*The many faces of Raymond Burr, from his films: Affair in Havana, Rear Window, Godzilla-King of Monsters, A Place in the Sun, and Crime of Passion.*

*There were 271 episodes of Perry Mason, and in all of those court battles, Perry Mason only lost three cases.*

*A fan-favorite scene from The Thing from Another World.*

*Actress, Sharon Tate in 1967. She was the first person murdered by the Charles Manson cult.*

# Reflections Part I

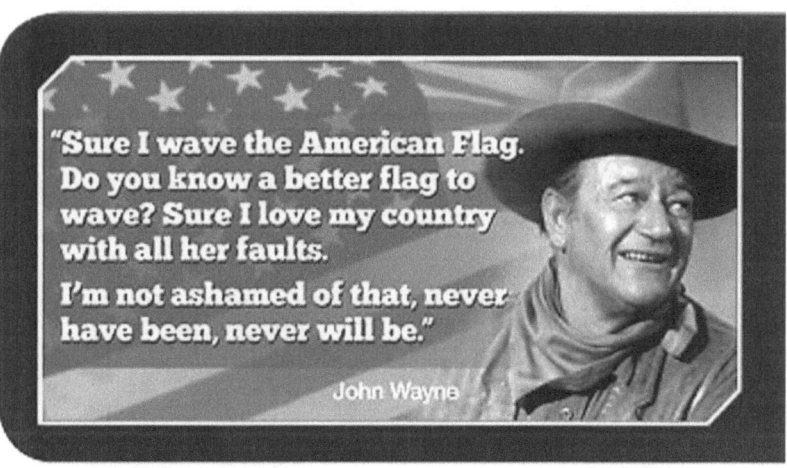

*John Wayne in a movie poster for Shepherd of the Hills.*

*They created the sound of Godzilla's roar by rubbing a pine tarcoated leather glove over a double bass string.*

*Just filming a scene in Godzilla!*

"We all go a little mad sometimes"—
Norman Bates The face that
scared a nation of movie-goers!

Before his variety show was
named the Ed Sullivan Show, it
was the Toast of the Town.

Alfred Hitchcock giving direction to
Anthony Perkins and Janet Leigh.

A humorous (but completely serious) sign
in the lobby outside of the Pycho movie.

Sadly, the '60s also saw the end of Clark Gable's films. In 1961, he died of a heart attack while he was filming, The Misfits. He was already sick and insisted on doing his own stunts, which added stress to the ailing Gable. Symona Boniface, commonly seen in Three Stooges films passed away on September 2, 1950. Other actors lost during that time included George Bernard Shaw, Edgar Rice Burroughs, Bull Montana, Noel Francis, Helen Parrish, and Billie Holiday.

Part 2

Rockin' in the '50s and '60s

In several ways, the film industry influenced rock n' roll in the '50s and '60s. The two professions seemed to interlope throughout the years. Actor Tony Curtis was known for a curl that he wore in front called the "ducktail curl." Elvis Presley copied that hairstyle. Ricky Nelson (a teen favorite) played his first song for the music world in John Wayne's film, Rio Bravo. The TV also played a major part in promoting rock & roll. A favorite among those TV programs was the introduction of the show, The Toast of the Town, on June 20, 1948. The guests on that first episode included Dean Martin and Jerry Lewis, Rodgers and Hammerstein, a pianist, a ballerina, a group of firemen that were humming and singing softly, and a boxing referee whose next gig was the Joe Louis-Jersey Joe Wolcott match. The critics did not like the show and predicted it not to last long. They were mostly turned off by the wide variety of acts. It was too much for them. However, the viewers across the country loved the show and continued to tune in every Sunday to watch the performers, which always included a music act. In 1955, the name changed to The Ed Sullivan Show.

Many Americans loved the show; from the way Sullivan stammered his words to the support he gave to new acts trying to find their spot among the fans. Sullivan was an ace in predicting who had true talent and who would go far. Appearing on his show gave people a chance to become stars overnight, that includes Joan Rivers, Carol Burnett, The Mamas and the Papas, Steppenwolf, The Beach Boys, Albert Schweitzer, Irving Berlin, and Dinah Shore. Regardless of the critics' opinions, fans enjoyed the variety of acts on the show. With as fun as Ed Sullivan was to watch, he also had his share of feuds offstage. Several stemmed from musicians that refused to change the lyrics to their songs – lyrics that Sullivan thought were too extreme for television, or as he called them "raucous."

Buddy Holly was one of the musicians who found himself in a feud with Ed Sullivan. Some say that Holly got the worst of Sullivan's bad side. Buddy Holly appeared on the show twice. His second – and last time - was on January 26, 1958. He was scheduled to sing, "Oh Boy." Before the show, Sullivan asked him to choose a different song to sing or change the lyrics. Holly refused, mostly because he already informed his friends and family that he would be singing the song on the show. Sullivan walked away mad. But there was more to come with those two.

Before the start of the show, Sullivan called the band together for a last-minute rehearsal, but the Crickets did now show, it was just Buddy Holly. When Sullivan inquired about where they were, Holly stated, "I don't know. No telling." Sullivan then said, "Well, I guess The Crickets are not too excited to be on The Ed Sullivan Show." Holly responded once more, stating, "I hope they're damn more excited than I am." Sullivan walked away, feeling even angrier. He chose then to cut their act down to one song.

When it was time came for Buddy Holly to take to the stage, Ed Sullivan introduced "Buddy Hollet and his Crickets" - purposefully mispronouncing his name. He also had the amplifier to his guitar turned off. Holly realized that it was off and played harder during the solo part of the song so that people watching can see that the technical difficulty was not coming from his end. Holly was furious with Sullivan. A few months later Sullivan invited him back onto his show. Holly refused and said Sullivan could not pay him enough money to go on there again.

When the Doors appeared on the show in 1967, they planned to sing "Light My Fire." The song was #1 on the charts. The Producer approached them a few minutes before they were supposed to go on stage. He told them they could not sing the word "higher" because of the context of the word in the song. The band was pretty angry, especially Jim Morrison. He told them they can still sing the song, just change that one word. Ray Manzarek, who played the keyboards, diffused the situation by agreeing to replace the word. Only when they went out, they sang the song as it was written – no changes. Sullivan, who was a stickler for following the rules, was furious and banned them from ever performing on the show again. The band learned then that they were scheduled for five more appearances, but those were gone now. Morrison's response was, "Hey, that's okay. We just did the Ed Sullivan show."

Some musicians were okay with Sullivan's censorship. On Elvis Presley's last performance, he was filmed from the waist up because of his shaking hips. The Rolling Stones agreed to put on suit jackets before going onstage, though they did try to argue it. Mick Jagger also changed the line in his song, "Let's Spend the Night Together" to say "Let's spend some time together." He let his annoyance at that quite known as he rolled his eyes after each line. Ed Sullivan never liked Elvis and never planned on putting him on his show. He hated his vibrating hips and thought his music was vulgar. However, Steve Allen had Presley on his show, and it was such a rating smash with the fans that Sullivan knew that he could not pass on sharing some of that success. This was especially since that episode clobbered the Ed Sullivan Show in the ratings. Elvis made three appearances on the Ed Sullivan Show. Bob Dylan was not one to get caught in his fury and have his name added to Sullivan's banned list. When he was invited to the show and then asked to change the words to his song also, he declined to appear. The song he wanted to sing was, "Talkin John Birch Paranoid Blues." The line he had a problem with was "Now Eisenhower, he's a Russian spy/ Lincoln, Jefferson, and that Roosevelt guy." They wanted him to change that to, "To my knowledge, there's just one man that's really a true American: George Lincoln Rockwell."

It was not just the musicians that would feel Sullivan's anger. Comedian, Jackie Mason, would also feel the sting. He appeared on the show in 1963. However, the show was preempted by President Johnson, meaning the acts would be cut short. During his stand-up comedy sketch, Sullivan was motioning for him to hurry up. Mason, gave several gestures back to Sullivan, all the while, he continued his act. Sullivan was not happy about his sarcasm and accused him of ignoring his request to cut his routine. He then banned Mason from the show for two years.

It was not all negative, though. Sullivan was a fighter for Civil Rights and gave ample air time to African Americans. Some of those musical acts include James Brown, Lena Horne, Louis Armstrong, The Jackson 5, Dizzy Gillespie, Eartha Kitt, and The Supremes. Actress Diahann Carroll once said that she owes a great deal of her success to the Ed Sullivan show. Viewers did not gracefully accept this. Every week he received dozens of letters, threatening him and warning him to stop. Sullivan knew he was doing the right thing and continued without a care about them.

One of the show's greatest episodes was when he brought the Beatles on for their first appearance. Ed Sullivan saw the Beatles a year earlier at an airport in England. The band was coming home from a show, and their fans greeted them with screams and cheers. That impressed Sullivan who just had to know who that band was! In December 1963, Walter Cronkite introduced the Beatles to America on his radio show. Teens went wild for the Fab Four, and by February their song, "I Want to Hold Your Hand" rocketed to the #1 spot on the charts.

On January 29th, Jack Paar played a video of the Beatles singing. However, it was more to laugh at them. He also said in jest, "It's nice to know that England has finally risen to our cultural level." He thought the band was a joke and would never be accepted in America. He thought for sure the Beatles would fade out. But not in Ed Sullivan's opinion. Less than two weeks later, he brought the Beatles to America. Paar even called in a few favors to get tickets to the show – at the request of his children.

When the Beatles made their debut on the Ed Sullivan on February 9, 1964, it would make music history! That night over 73 million people tuned in to watch the Beatles. That was a little over half of the country's population at the time. During that two-hour episode that showed the Beatles, not a single crime was committed across the country. That was the night Beatlemania was born in the United States. They almost went on that night without George Harrison. He caught tonsillitis and had a fever of 102 degrees. But Harrison said there was no way he was going to miss the opportunity. The Beatles made eight more appearances on the show.

Also, performing that night was 19-year-old Davy Jones. He was in the cast of Oliver as the "Artful Dodger." The entire cast was on the show, and he sang, "I'd Do Anything" with Jones in the lead vocals. Before that night, Jones never heard of the Beatles.

Things came to a sudden end for Sullivan when CBS hired Fred Silverman to manage daytime television. Silverman's first decision was to do a "rural purge," ending any show that was aimed towards rural audiences. Along with Sullivan's show, he also canceled The Beverly Hillbillies, Green Acres, and Hogan Heroes. The decision to cancel the Ed Sullivan Show came after they finished filming their 24th season and were on a summer break. It was unexpected to everyone, including Sullivan. He was always disappointed that he did not get to film a farewell episode.

The Ed Sullivan Show ran from June 20, 1948 – June 6, 1971, producing a total of 1,068 episodes. In spite of the show's rocky start and the critic's poor opinion of it, the Ed Sullivan Show would become the longest-running show in TV history and the only variety show to air in four decades. In the 23 years that the show was on the air, it maintained the same time slot – Sundays at 8:00 on CBS. Ed Sullivan paved the way for night time talk shows and variety shows alike.

Part 3

The Birth of Rock n' Roll

Alan Freed is a staple in the pages of music history. He was a Cleveland DJ who, in 1952, coined the phrase "Rock & Roll" as it pertains to music. The expression was used before in regards to sex. Several sources consider the song "Rocket 88" to be the first rock & roll song. It was recorded in 1951 by Ike Turner and sung by Jackie Brenston. Freed is responsible for several successes in music. He also played a role in desegregation by encouraging children of all races to listen to 'rock & roll' music. Many exclaimed that Ohio DJ "put Cleveland on the map and Rock & Roll on the radio."

*When Elvis Presley sang on the Ed Sullivan the second time he was filmed from the chest up because his dance moves were considered vulgar.*

*John Lennon and the Quarrymen singing at Woolton Parish Church on July 6, 1957. In the audience was his soon-to-be music partner, Paul McCartney.*

*Reflections Part I*

*Jerry Allison, top, Buddy Holly, center, and Joe Maulden, bottom, as The Crickets.*

*The Beatles arriving at John F Kennedy International Airport on February 7, 1964.*

On March 21, 1952, Freed organized the rock & roll show - Moondog Coronation Ball. It starred Dominoes, Paul Williams and the Hucklebuckers, Tiny Grimes and the Rocking Highlanders, Danny Cobb, Varetta Dillard, and other artists. It was the first-ever rock & roll concert.

Elvis Presley had one of the biggest impacts on the sound of rock & roll. Sam Phillips discovered Presley in 1954. He first met 19-year-old Elvis when he walked into Sun Studio to make a record for his mother, Gladys. He paid $4 to record the song, "That's All Right Mama." Phillips kept in touch with Elvis since he often stopped by to talk to him and his assistant, Marion Keisker. Phillips signed him on after he recorded a second song with him.

Colonel Tom Parker (not a real colonel) managed several country singers in Memphis and when he heard about Sun Studio's up-and-coming star he was determined to work with him. In 1956, Parker arranged for the sale of Presley's contract from Sun to RCA. This move officially made him Elvis Presley's manager. A position that he would hold for the next two decades. Many people did not like the way Parker managed his career and accused him of holding Elvis back creatively. They also claimed he took too much money from him. At times, he would receive 50% of his earnings.

It was Mae Boren Axton who would have one of the most significant impacts on Elvis Presley's career. Axton was a songwriter in Comanche, Oklahoma. She was the one who introduced Elvis to Colonel Parker. Axton later pressured RCA Victor to give Elvis a recording deal. From the moment she met Elvis, she saw great promise in him as a singer. She told him, "You need a million-seller, and I'm going to write it for you." She would go on to do just that when she wrote, "Heartbreak Hotel."

Heartbreak Hotel would be his breakthrough hit. A newspaper article about suicide inspired the song. Tommy Durden, who played the steel guitar for Elvis, read an article about a man who killed himself by jumping from a hotel window. In his suicide note, there was only one sentence: "I walk a lonely street." Durden took the article to Axton to see if together they can write a song from that. It only took Durden and Axton an hour to write the song, Elvis did change one of the lines. He turned "they pray to die" to "they could die."

Producers at RCA had doubts about the song because it did not sound like his other songs. They implored him to go back and change it, but he stood by the song, and they agreed to move forward with it. They released the song on January 27, 1956, just days after his 21$^{st}$ birthday. He quickly earned the name, "the King of Rock & Roll."

## Reflections Part I

Elvis had come a long way. He bought his first guitar when he was just 11 years old. His mother took him to Tupelo Hardware to buy him a bicycle for his birthday. When Elvis saw a rifle for sale, he decided he wanted that instead. His mother didn't feel comfortable with the idea of buying her 11-year-old son a gun. They compromised, and he got a guitar instead. Forest Bobo remembers the day he sold the guitar to Gladys for $7.90. He wanted a rifle, but his mother convinced him to get a guitar instead. When Elvis was 12 years old, a local radio show offered him a chance to sing live on air. Elvis declined because he was too shy to go on. Two years before Elvis recorded his first album, he auditioned for a gospel quartet named the Songfellows. They turned Elvis down.

Throughout his career, Elvis put on several benefit concerts. One of those concerts raised $50,000 to complete the building of the USS Arizona Memorial in Hawaii. More than 1,100 soldiers died on the USS Arizona in the attack on Pearl Harbor. He performed several concerts in Canada but never held concerts in any other country, even though he had fans around the world. Parker turned down hundreds of offers because he was hiding a secret that he feared would come out. Parker was an illegal immigrant. He was born Andreas Cornelis van Kuijk, in the Netherlands. He was afraid that if his real identity came out when they were overseas that they might not let him back in the country.

On May 5, 1975, Elvis gave a charity concert in Jackson, Mississippi, to raise money for those who suffered damage from a tornado that swept through McComb, Mississippi. After the show, Elvis gave an additional $100,000 to then-Governor Bill Waller to distribute to the families, as well.

Elvis became known for his smooth voice, curled lip, and shaking hips that made the girls scream. His signature black hair was dyed. It was originally brown. Before he dyed it, he made it black by using shoe polish. He was also known for his extreme generosity. He lavished friends and strangers with jewelry, cash, and gifts. Elvis, who was a quiet introvert, grew up poor so he empathized with people that he thought could use some help. These are just a few of his acts of kindness.

*He bought houses for a few friends and even paid for two of their weddings. His aid, Lamar Fike, was one of the lucky to receive a house.

He went in person to deliver a new wheelchair to a disabled woman when he found out that she could not afford one.

On Mother's Day, in 1971, he gave flowers to all of the female employees at the International Hotel in Las Vegas.

*Elvis starred in several films. On the first day of production, he lavished his female co-stars with flowers. On the last day of filming, Frankie and Johnny, he bought the entire cast and crew a watch designed by jeweler Harry Levitch, depicting a cross and a Jewish star.

*Elvis's favorite book was The Impersonal Life. He gave several copies to people who were important to him.

*Once a friend was visiting him, and he told him he like the motorcycle that he had parked outside. Elvis threw the keys to him and told him to "take it."

*Another friend once admired the shirt he was wearing, so he took the shirt off his back and gave it to him.

*When he was drafted into the army he bought everyone in his unit an extra set of fatigues. He also donated his salary, of $74 a month, to charity.

*He gave away so much jewelry that it is impossible to keep track of it all. There were times when he traveled with his personal jeweler, Lowell Hayes, just in case he felt like giving away jewelry. He gave another friend $100,000 worth of jewelry. In 1974, 5-year-old, Rhonda Williams was at an Elvis concert with her mom. When Elvis spotted her, he took off his cross necklace and hung it around her neck.

*He often purchased items to donate to charity auctions. In December 1961, he started a holiday tradition of donating checks to 50 different charities. One of those checks went to Memphis Mayor Henry Loeb. It was a $50,000 check that Loeb was given to pass out to numerous charities.

*In 1965, Elvis bought a yacht for $55,000 that once belonged to Franklin Roosevelt. The yacht, which dubbed the name the Potomac, was built in 1935 specifically for Roosevelt. After owning the Potomac for a few months, he donated it to St Jude's hospital so they could sell it to raise money.

*He gave away over 200 Cadillacs to friends, family, and even a few strangers. He also gave one to his dentist. Once he was at the bank when the bank teller mentioned that her birthday was in two days. On the morning of her birthday, she too received a Cadillac. He gave a Cadillac to a maid when he heard that she had to walk a mile every morning to reach the nearest bus stop. He bought a car for his karate instructor, Ed Parker. (Then he bought Parker's wife a $12,000 mink coat.)

Those are just some of his acts of kindness. There are dozens more, though only a few people knew. Elvis said there was one significant reason he gave away all of those gifts, that he called happies. It was that he loved seeing how happy he could make people. Some of the gifts were given in honor of their loyalty. Some were just to show his love for friends and family. There were also a few times when those gifts were an apology for something he did wrong. In 1967, in honor of Elvis's generosity to so many charities, Memphis Mayor William Ingram and Tennessee Governor Buford Ellington declared October 29th "Elvis Presley Day" in Tennessee.

# Part 4

## Making of Motown

On January 12, 1959, Berry Gordy opened his music production company, Tamla Records. Outside the United States, they were known as Tamla Motown, then later as Motown. Gordy created the name Motown from the words "Motor City," the nickname of Michigan – which is also where the Motown company was born. They earned the name Motor City after the ford Motor plant opened there. At one time, Gordy worked at the Ford plant. Gordy was also a great songwriter. He wrote over 200 songs including "I Want You Back" for Jackson 5, "Do You Love Me" for the Contours and "Money" for the Beatles. Gordy started the company with $800 that he borrowed from his father.

Motown released their first record in 1961. The song was Shop Around by the Miracles. A few months later they released "Please Mr. Postman" by the Marvelettes. It was the company's first number one song.

The musicians worked just as hard to promote Motown Records as Gordy did. He had his own "charm school" to teach his musicians etiquette that included poise, grace, and mannerisms. The musicians were also encouraged to dress in a high fashion image to motivate other African-American musicians. They also promoted their music when possible. Before the Supremes became famous, Diana Ross used to carry around a small record player so that she could play her record for others. They monitored their other activities and careers. At one point, Marvin Gaye wanted to play on the Detroit Lions team, but Motown did not want to see him out there getting knocked around.

Motown had their own backup band that played on almost all of their records. That band was the Funk Brothers. They signed on with Motown from its start in 1959. The Funk Brothers grew to be a powerhouse band and later recognized as one of the most successful studio bands in music history. They were made up of musicians from blues and jazz clubs. The 13 original members of the Funk Brothers included:

Joe Hunter and Earl van Dyke (keyboards)
Clarence Isabell (double bass)
James Jamerson (bass guitar and double bass)
Benny "Papa Zita" Benjamin and Richard "Pistol Allen (drums)
Paul Riser (trombone)
Jack Ashford (trombone, percussion, vibraphone, marimba)
Robert White, Eddie Willis, and Joe Messina (guitar)
Eddie "Bongo" Brown (percussion)
Jack Brokensha (vibraphone, marimba)

Eddie Wills described how he made his first guitar by attaching broom wire to the house. The Funk Brothers played for Motown from 1959 – 1972. They played on every song recorded during those years. Earl van Dyke never got along with Diana Ross. He called it an intense dislike. The band was instrumental in developing the Motown sound and never received proper credit. They were never featured on an album cover, and they were never invited to tour with the musicians.

*Reflections Part I*

The youngest performers to sign with Motown were the Jackson 5 and 11-year-old Stevie Wonder. Motown discovered many musicians. They include:

Rick James
The Contours
Marvin Gaye
The Four Tops
The Temptations
The Marvelettes
The Isley Brothers
Gladys Knight and the Pips
Martha Reeves and the Vandellas
Smokey Robinson & the Miracles
The Supremes, Diana Ross (solo)
The Commodores, Lionel Richie (solo)

In the '50s and '60s, the world of rock & roll was introduced to a new wave of girl bands. There were usually 3 or 4 members in a girl band. Their music was a mixture of doo-wop harmonies with rhythm and blues. The girls were not given the same respect and recognition that the guys received. For example, the Supremes were called the Primettes initially and were formed to be the sister group to the Temptations. However, the members were changed often over the years. Two of them were let go for getting pregnant. Most people do not know that they performed on the Ed Sullivan show 20 times. It was the most of any other music group. Some of the favorite girl bands of that time include:

The Bobbettes
The Shirelles
The Cookies
The Deltairs
The Teddy Bears
The Chantels
The Supremes
The Paris Sisters
The Ronettes
The Blossoms

The Shangri Las
The Exciters
The Marveletes
The Chiffons
The Silhouettes
Martha & the Vandellas

Another type of music was called "answer songs." These songs are written as a reply to another musician's song. The song "Got a Job" was in response to the Silhouettes' #1 hit "Get a Job." There were more just like that!
*The Kitty Wells song, "It Wasn't God Who Made Honky Tonk Angels" was a reply song to Hank Thompson's hit "The Wild Side of Life." *Jody Miller's song, "Queen of the House," was a reply song to Roger Miller's hit "King of the Road." *Thelma Carpenter's song, "Yes I'm Lonesome Tonight," was a reply song to Elvis Presley's "Are You Lonesome Tonight."

*The Temptations' song, "My Girl," was a reply song to Mary Wells' hit, "My Guy."

*Carla Thomas' song, "I'll Bring it Home to You," was a reply song to Sam Cooke's hit, "Bring it on Home to Me."

The 1950s brought in a vast myriad of musicians and bands, all introducing new styles, new dance moves, and new rhythms. The pioneers of Rock n' Roll include Elvis Presley, Bill Haley, Buddy Holly, and Little Richard.

Bill Haley got his first guitar when he was a teenager. He made one out of cardboard and pretended to play it, so his parents replaced it with a real one. He named his band Bill Haley and the Comets after the famous comet. For their first few shows, they were only paid $1 a night. When they released "Rock Around the Clock" in 1954, it became the first rock and roll song to sell a million copies. And Bill Haley became known as the Father of Rock & Roll. As Haley was setting the tone for rock and roll, following close behind him was 19-year-old Buddy Holly. When Holly was 17-years-old, he formed his first band with his friend Bob Montgomery. They were called Buddy and Bob. Two years later on February 13, 1955, Buddy and Bob opened for Elvis Presley at Fair Park Coliseum in Lubbock, Texas.

In, 1957, Buddy Holly formed the band, "The Crickets" and they released "Peggy Sue." The song was written by Holly, Norman Petty, and Jerry

Allison. It was first titled, "Cindy Lou" after Buddy Holly's niece. Allison asked them to change it to "Peggy Sue" after his girlfriend. Their next release was "That'll Be the Day." It was their only song to reach the top ten. They went on to record seven more songs that made it to the top 50.

The original members of the Crickets left in 1958. Holly kept the Crickets and replaced them with Tommy Allsup (guitar), Carl Bunch (drums), and Waylon Jennings (bass guitar). They were selected to headline the Winter Dance Party that was touring 24 cities in the Midwest. Along with the Crickets, the Winter Dance Party included Dion and the Belmonts, Ritchie Valens, and the Big Bopper.

The tour began on January 23, 1959. They were initially traveling by bus. It was a harsh cold winter, and the heater on the bus broke down. Holly's drummer ended up in the hospital with frostbite, and several members of the tour caught the flu. Holly decided to charter a plane on February 23$^{rd}$ to fly them from Clear Lake, Iowa to Fargo, North Dakota. It would have been a fast flight; they only had to travel across the border.

It was a small plane, and there was only room for three of them. Since Holly chartered the plane, he was getting one of the seats. Waylon Jennings had one of them, but he gave it to JP Richardson (the Big Bopper) because he was one of the men that caught the flu. Holly did not want Jennings to give up his seat, and they even argued about it. There was a coin toss to see who would get the third seat and Dion DiMucci won it. But when he found out that it cost $36, he said that was too much and gave the seat to Ritchie Valens.

Shortly after takeoff, a windy snowstorm caused the plane to crash back to the ground, killing everyone on board – the three musicians and the pilot. Rock and Roll was still in its infancy, and now three of their brightest stars were gone. This dark day in music history came to be known as the day the music died.

On his tombstone, Buddy's last name is spelled "Holley." When he signed his first record deal with Decca Records in 1956, they accidentally misspelled his name as "Holly." He never corrected them and let them keep that spelling.

Over a decade later, the pain of losing these great musicians was still a sore spot for many. Don McLean was one of them. He released his feelings through a song he wrote in tribute to the musicians on board the plane that day. He titled the song "American Pie" after the name of the airplane that the men were flying on that day. One of the lines in the song was "I can't remember if I cried when I read about his widowed bride." That was in tribute to Holly's widow, Maria Elena Holly. She was pregnant with their first child when he died. She had a miscarriage the next day.

Throughout music history, many people credit Holly with creating the sound of rock and roll. One thing we do know is that without Buddy Holly and the Crickets we would not have had the Beatles. Well, that would not be their name anyway. John Lennon chose the name because he wanted an insect name like how Buddy Holly did it. When John Lennon was a teen in his group the Quarrymen, Buddy Holly was his biggest influence. In fact, when John Lennon and Paul McCartney met at a church picnic, John Lennon was onstage singing Buddy Hull's song, "That'll Be the Day." Lennon later explained that after picking the name the Beetles he changed the spelling to be a mix of music and the insect. In an interview in 1964, he stated, "It was beat and beetles, and when you said it people thought of crawly things, and when you read it, it was beat music."

And without the Beatles the history of rock and roll and the sound of music today would be extremely different. The Beatles got their start in 1956 as the Quarrymen. John Lennon started the band, and it included Rod Davis, Len Garry, Colin Hanton, John Duff Lowe, and Chas Newby. On July 6, 1957, the Quarrymen were playing at St. Peter's Church in Woolton, Liverpool. Paul McCartney was in the audience that day. Later that afternoon, Lennon and McCartney were introduced to each other by a mutual friend. McCartney impressed Lennon when he tuned his guitar. A week later, Lennon asked him to join the Quarrymen. The next member to join the Quarrymen was George Harrison, followed by Stuart Sutcliffe. In 1960, they changed their name to the Beatles. At that time the band consisted of John Lennon, Paul McCartney, George Harrison, and Stuart Sutcliffe on guitar. Pete Best was their drummer.

During a show in Hamburg, they played at a rough club, and a fight broke up while they were onstage. They took off running from the building, and Stuart Sutcliffe was pulled into the brawl. They dragged him to the ground and kicked him repeatedly. He was kicked several times in the head. John Lennon and Pete Best went back to pull him away. He begged Sutcliffe to go to the hospital, but he refused. When they got home his fiancé, Astrid Kirchherr, also pleaded with him to seek medical attention but he insisted that he would be okay. On Tuesday, April 10, 1962, Stuart died from a brain hemorrhage. Several months before his death, Sutcliffe suffered from debilitating headaches. Doctors are confident that the hemorrhage was brought on from the injuries he received that night. They do not know who delivered the kick to his head that would later kill him. Many Beatles fans remember Sutcliffe as the Fifth Beatle.

In 1961, the Beatles sang, as the Beat Brothers, in a backup on Tony Sheridan's song, "My Bonnie." During that time, Brian Epstein's family-owned NEMS Record Store on Great Charlotte Street. Their philosophy was that if they do not have the album that you are looking for, they will get it. Well, a few months after Tony Sheridan and the Beat Brothers released "My Bonnie," 18-year-old Raymond Jones went into NEMS looking for the album. Brian Epstein was working that day. However, they did not have the record and had never heard of them. Jones told Epstein all about the Beatles, who played in the Cavern, a couple of blocks away from NEMS. That week Epstein went down to meet the Beatles. He was immediately drawn to the Beatles. Within the weeks that followed he was signed on as the Beatles manager.

The first thing he did was to change their appearance and behavior on stage. The Beatles already had their mop-top haircut, thanks to Sutcliffe's fiancé Kirchherr. She was a Cosmetology student and gave the boys their famous haircut as part of her homework. She was practicing giving haircuts, and the Beatles volunteered to let her practice on them. They liked the cut she made and kept it. Epstein did not want to change the hairstyle, just their clothes. It was his idea for them to wear a suit and tie on stage. They resisted at first, preferring to wear their leather jackets. He also told them there would not be anymore smoking, swearing, or drinking alcohol.

In 1962, the Beatles met Ringo Starr who played drums for Rory Storm and the Hurricanes. Pete Best was the drummer for the Beatles but was often missing shows because he was sick. Each time he missed an appearance, they would borrow Ringo from the Hurricanes. Eventually, Epstein was fed up and encouraged the Beatles to fire Best and hire Ringo full time. Ringo was happy to join the Beatles. And on August 18, 1962, it was official, Ringo Starr was now a Beatle. He played drums during their concert that night at Hulme Hall in Birkenhead, England – and the rest is rock and roll history.

In late 1966, Kenny and his friend Bobby were cruising in Kenny's 57 Chevy headed for Blanchard, listening to music the whole way. "The Devil with the Blue Dress" by Mitch Ryder and the Detroit Wheels came on the radio, catching Bobby's attention as he suddenly exclaimed, "Listen to that!" Kenny heard bits and pieces of Mitch Ryder's music previously but did not pay much attention to them. But after that day, Mitch Ryder was his favorite!

Mitch Ryder was born, William Levise Jr. His father was a musician, so you can say that music was in his blood. When he was a teen, Ryder sang for the soul group, Peps. The rest of the members of Peps were African-American, and because of racial tension, they asked Ryder to leave the group. Shortly after that, he formed his own band – Tempest, along with his friends from school. They also sang soul music at the club, the Village. No one is sure how long that band lasted, but Jennings was soon singing lead in the group, Billy Lee & The Rivieras. Along with Jennings, this group included John Badanjek on drums, Mark Manko on lead guitar, Joe Kubert on rhythm guitar, Jim McCarty on lead guitar, and Jim McAllister on bass.

When they met record producer, Bob Crewe, of DynoVoice Records, he knew the band had promise and wanted to launch their music career, after making a few changes. One of those changes was to change the name of the group to Mitch Ryder & the Detroit Wheels. They released their first album as in Mitch Ryder & the Detroit Wheels 1965. Their biggest hits included Devil With a Blue Dress On, Sock it to Me Baby, and Jenny Take a Ride. Their song, "Ring My Bell," was banned from radio stations in several states. It was said to have sexual innuendos. In 1978, Ryder took a break from music because of problems with his throat. For several years after that, he spent his time painting and writing. That did not last long. Nothing can hold a Detroit singer down.

*Reflections Part I*

## *Did you know?*

- *Elvis Presley failed music class in high school.*

- *John Wayne enjoyed the game of chess so much that when he was on set, they kept his trailer stocked with alcohol and a chessboard. He used to hang up a sign that said, "Do You Want to Play Chess with John Wayne?"*

- *Every time Beethoven sat down to write music, he poured ice water over his head.*

- *When Beethoven was challenged to an improvisation duel by one of his rivals named Steibelt, Beethoven took a piece of Steibelt's music, turned it upside-down then played it, Then he improvised on that theme for over an hour. Steibelt left halfway through.*

- *Frank Sinatra described the Beatles song "Something" as the greatest love song ever written.*

*Two Japanese planes shot down at the same time at Guadalcanal.*

*Henderson Field at Guadalcanal.*

# Chapter 6

## Part 1 America at War
## World War II - War for the Pacific

When the year 1940 rolled around, America was enjoying over 20 years of peacetime. The United States had not been to war since November 11, 1918. That was the day that World War I came to an end. It would be over two decades later, on Friday, September 1, 1939, when the next war broke out – World War II. The countries that fought in the war were divided into sections. There was the "Axis" comprised of Germany, Italy, and Japan. Fighting against them were the "Allies." That included the United States of America, Britain, France, Australia, Canada, New Zealand, India, the Soviet Union, and China. It was a complete accident that the first United States soldier killed in the war, was shot by a Russian.

As the fighting in World War II grew, there were two main sections of battle. One part of the war took place in Europe against Italy and Nazi Germany. The other took place in the Pacific and was chiefly between the United States and Japan. The battles among the Pacific Islands also came to be known as the Pacific Campaign.

The confidence of the Japanese came from the strong artillery that they were armed with, which included several large battleships. The Yamato, Musashi, and Shinano were going to be the first three of their mammoth battleships. However, after the battle of Midway, the Shinano (which was partially built) was converted to a carrier. The Yamato and Musashi remained the largest battleships ever built. A 300-ton overhead crane was used to assemble the heaviest parts. The guns were 70 feet long. The diameter of the shells was 18 inches and could travel up to 26 miles. They weighed in at 3200 lbs. They had planned to build five Yamato Class Battleships, but the battle of Midway changed their plans.

Musashi was sunk at the Battle of Leyte Gulf on October 24, 1944. On April 7th,1945, the Yamato and it's nine escort ships were attacked by an American fleet of 60 ships and 400 planes. Yamato and her escorts had no air support against the massive attack. After 19 torpedoes struck the Yamato, it exploded. The battleship ascended more than 2,000 feet, killing 2,498 soldiers.

The Shinano was rushed into combat as an aircraft carrier in November 1944 before its construction was fully completed. It sunk ten days later, on November 29, 1944, when the USS Archerfish submarine hit the gigantic carrier with four torpedoes. Shinano was the largest naval vessel to be sunk by a submarine!

The War for the Pacific all began when Japan attacked Pearl Harbor. They had tried for some time to coax America into joining the fighting of World War II. They were confident that they had the power to conquer the United States. The United States did not join the war until 1941 after the Japanese bombed Pearl Harbor. It happened on December 7, 1941, at 7:55 am, the Japanese aircraft filled the sky in a sneak attack on Pearl Harbor, on the island of Oahu, Hawaii. In less than two hours bombs and bullets rained down from 353 Japanese aircraft. They destroyed/damaged 21 U.S. warships and 188 of our aircraft. They also killed 2,403 American soldiers and civilians and wounded another 1,000, approximately.

At 8:10 am, an 1,800-pound bomb crashed through the deck of the USS Arizona. The ship exploded and sank, killing 1,000 men who could not escape. A sailor named Joe George was on the USS Vestal (a repair ship) that was tied to the Arizona. George had gotten into a fight on Friday, December 5th, so he had his weekend leave taken away. Otherwise, he would not have been there mopping the decks of the Vestal when the attack began. George disobeyed an order to cut loose from the Arizona so he could rescue the last six survivors. He was never acknowledged for his actions that day because he never talked about what happened. It was years later when a member of his family started researching his time at Peal Harbor when they learned of his heroic efforts.

## Reflections Part I

There were several unsung heroes that day. One was Private Ed Minford who was on kitchen detail that day. He and several others spotted something on the horizon, that looked similar to a massive storm cloud. By the time they realized it was enemy planes, they were already upon them. The men started running down the halls, banging and screaming for the others to wake up. The saved the lives of many men who otherwise would have been asleep in bed.

The next battleship to be struck was the USS Oklahoma, affectionately called "Okie" by her crew. Eight torpedoes hit the ship in 12 minutes. It rolled onto its side before sinking. There were 429 soldiers killed aboard the Oklahoma, and another 32 soldiers rescued. The Oklahoma was the Navy's oldest battleships. It was also the first one built that would burn fuel oil. For a battleship, this would save weight and volume of displacement.

The battleships destroyed that day were the USS Arizona, USS Oklahoma, USS California, USS West Virginia, USS Utah, USS Maryland, USS Pennsylvania, and the USS Tennessee. The USS Nevada was left with significant damage. Except for the USS Arizona, USS Oklahoma, and the USS Utah, the ships were later salvaged and repaired. The USS Utah was the first battleship destroyed that morning.

In the days leading up to Pearl Harbor, the position of Commander in Chief of the United States Fleet went by the anagram name CINCUS. Yes, that is pronounced "sink us." The man that held that title was Husband Edward Kimmel. Shortly after the attack, that name changed from CINCUS to COMINCH. Ten days after the attack, he was relieved of his duties. He was demoted in rank from a four-star admiral to the two-star rank of rear admiral. Just a few months after the attack, Admiral Kimmel retired from the Navy.

Kimmel was born and raised in Kentucky. His father, Major Manning Marius Kimmel, fought in the Civil War. He first served on the side of the Union soldiers. He later switched his loyalties to the Confederate Army so that he could serve alongside his friends and family. American citizens were outraged over the attack and united in President Roosevelt's decision to declare war on Japan. If it was a fight they wanted, America was ready to give it to them. We were not alone. Canada was also furious at what they did. In fact, because of the attack, Canada declared war against Japan before America did.

There were quite a few battles among the islands in the Pacific. The Japanese fought hard to seize control of several countries and islands. The Allies fought just as hard to prevent that from happening.

Part 2

Battle of Wake Island
December 8, 1941 - December 23, 1941

In the Central Pacific Ocean, just 600 miles west of Hawaii, are a trio of islands, the Wilkes, Peale, and Wake. In January 1941, the civilian firm, Contractors Pacific Naval Air Bases (CPNAB), began construction of American submarine and air bases on Wake Island. They were nearly complete when on December 8, 1941, just hours after the attack on Pearl Harbor, 36 Japanese Bombers attacked 449 U.S. Marines that were stationed on Wake Island. There were also 449 construction workers from CPNAB living on the island.

It was a short battle and was over on December 23$^{rd}$. However, this was a defeat for the Marines. The Japanese would retain control of the island until the end of the war. The 1,616 American soldiers that survived the battle were kept as prisoners of war and made to board a ship heading for China. While walking toward the ship, they were beaten with whips and clubs. The civilians were held on the island used as forced labor.

Sadly, on October 5, 1943, Japan was convinced the island was about to be raided once more, so they ordered the execution of the 98 American civilians captured during the Battle of Wake Island. The Japanese lined them up and started shooting them with machine guns. One of the prisoners escaped and returned to carve a memorial into a large rock that still stands today. That prisoner was later caught and executed.

On September 4, 1945, two days before the end of World War II, the Japanese surrendered the island back to the Americans. Today Wake Island is a U.S. Territory that is only used to house 150 military and civilian contractors. It is often an added site to Military Tours.

Part 3

Battle of the Coral Sea
May 4, 1942 - May 8, 1942

The Battle of the Coral Sea was another one of the shorter battles of World War II. It lasted from May 4, 1942 – May 8, 1942, and came to be known as the 4-Day War. This was the first battle ever to be fought from air-to-sea, meaning that aircraft was launched from carriers at sea.

The biggest loss for the Americans was having their battleship, USS Lexington fired upon by a Japanese airstrike. The Lexington was nicknamed the Blue Ghost because it was not camouflaged like their other ships. There were 216 crewmen on board the Lexington that were killed.

The Battle of the Coral Sea was an attempt to gain control of the Coral Sea by invading Port Moresby in southeast New Guinea. However, as they landed, they were ambushed American aircraft who learned of their plans by cracking their codes through intercepted messages. During this 4-day battle, the U.S. lost 543 troops, and the Japanese lost 1,074 soldiers. Almost all of the Japanese aircraft were destroyed, including their largest, Shoho, bringing their invasion to a halt. They also lost their largest aircraft carrier, Shokaku. The Japanese quickly retreated from the island, giving victory to the Allies. If they had achieved their goal in gaining control of the Coral Sea, this would have been a direct threat to Australia.

Part 4

Battle of Midway
June 4, 1942 - June 7, 1942

The Battle of Midway changed the direction of control over the Pacific Ocean between America and Japan. The battle started on June 4, 1942, just six months after the Attack on Pearl Harbor, and lasted until June 7$^{th}$. It was a strategic plan by the Japanese to lure the United States away from their base, out into the Pacific Ocean and then annihilate them. They wanted to remove the United States as a powerhouse in the war. Japan planned to beat America in the Battle of Midway and then move on to attack Fiji, Samoa, and to attack Hawaii again.

It was the events at Pearl Harbor that led Isoroku Yamamoto to devise the battle plan at Midway. Yamamoto was the commander-in-chief of the Combined Fleet of the Imperial Japanese Navy. He was also the chief architect behind the Attack at Pearl Harbor. He was so angry that some of the battleships were able to be salvaged from the wreckage left behind that he sought out to try and destroy them again. The island of Midway was an outpost for American troops at that time. It was yet another incentive for Yamamoto to annihilate the place and all of the soldiers stationed there. It was also out of range of American aircraft. However, the Japanese did not realize that military intelligence, known as American Cryptographers, (Allied Signals Intelligence

Units, also called Fleet radio Units) had cracked their code. They learned all of the details of the attack, including the exact date and time. They, in turn, warned the Navy of the planned ambush. Knowing that the Japanese were on their way, the Americans set out to find them first. Lt. Commander Wade McClusky Jr led the search for the Japanese fleet at Midway on the morning of June 4, 1942. Miraculously, he found the fleet just as he was about to give up on the search and return to the USS Enterprise. Instead, he began the attack as soon as he spotted them. His two small squadrons were able to catch the Japanese completely by surprise. The two Japanese carriers were quickly destroyed. When McClusky did return to his base, upon landing on the Enterprise, they found that he had been wounded. His plane only had one gallon of fuel and was riddled with 55 bullet holes.

The plan of the Japanese did not work out as expected. Instead, they were the ones defeated in the battle. Four Japanese aircraft carriers and a heavy cruiser were sunk, and 248 aircraft were destroyed. The Americans lost one aircraft carrier, one destroyer, and 150 aircraft. There were 307 American soldiers that died in the battle. However, the Japanese lost 3,057 soldiers, and 37 were captured.

Poor dispositions and underestimating the strength of the American military contributed to the loss of the Japanese in this battle. Interestingly, Yamamoto wanted to destroy the American aircraft that survived Pearl Harbor. But it was their four aircraft that were destroyed– the same four that they used against the Americans at Pearl Harbor. British military historian John Keegan stated that the American's victory in the Battle of Midway was "the most stunning and decisive blow in the history of naval warfare."

Part 5

Battle at Guadalcanal
August 7, 1942, - February 9, 1943

Guadalcanal is the main island that makes up the Solomon Islands. It was there that the Japanese planned to build a base. Construction began on June 8, 1942. Two months later, on August 7th, the United States Marines swooped in and launched a surprise attack against the Japanese, to seize control of the airbase that was still under construction. A base that they later named Henderson Field. The plans to raid Guadalcanal were relatively flimsy and became known as "Operation Shoestring." The day they rushed the island, they were only armed with ten days worth of ammunition and 60 days worth of food and fuel. More supplies had to be funneled in later. However, the Japanese were also not prepared for battle. They did not believe that the American troops had the know-how or power to reach them. But they were wrong! Every branch of the U.S. military fought in this battle – the Army, Navy, Marines, and Coast Guard. (The U.S. Navy was not established yet. That would happen two years after the end of World War II.)

During the war, a group of Marines were ambushed and had little chance of getting away. That was when Signalman First Class Douglas Munro, of the Coast Guard, swooped in and rescued them. This body of water was approximately 6-feet wide, and Munro was the only one that could maneuver his watercraft through it. Though he and his crew did rescue the Marines, the Japanese continued to fire upon them. Just before they reached the American side, Munro was shot in the base of his skull and died instantly. He was posthumously awarded the Medal of Honor. To this day, Munro is the only member of the U.S. Coast Guard to receive that medal.

Both sides suffered significant losses among their aircraft, including approximately 600 planes on both sides. It was the Japanese that lost the majority of their troops. A Japanese source stated over 40,000 Japanese soldiers and civilians died at Saipan. The Americans lost 3,426 soldiers. On February 9, 1943, the Japanese retreated and relinquished control over Guadalcanal to the allies. When they left the island, it was done so quietly that the American troops were unaware that they were alone.

Part 6

Battle of Saipan
June 15, 1944 - July 9, 1944

Among Japan's Mariana Islands is the island of Saipan. On June 15, 1944, the U.S. Marines charged onto the island to establish a much-needed airbase. With that airbase, they could then launch their new long-range B29 bombers directly at Japan's home islands. The Marines launched several pre-assault bombardments onto the island before storming the beaches. In their haste, they missed several Japanese gun emplacements along the beach cliffs. When they landed on the beach, they found themselves under a hail of bullets and exploding bombs. Over 2,000 Marines died on the first day of battle. They also suffered several hundred casualties from barbed wire traps and loosely covered trenches. One of the marines in that battle, John Chapin, described the events of that day in a book he later wrote, titled, "Breaching the Marianas: The Battle for Saipan."

> *"bodies lying in mangles and grotesque positions; blasted and burned out pillboxes; the burning wrecks of LVTs [landing vehicles]...; the acrid smell of high explosives; the shattered trees; and the churned up sand littered with discarded equipment."* - John Chapin

The battle grew particularly brutal near Mount Tapotchau, Saipan's highest peak. It was there that the Marines nicknamed the battle sites "Death Valley" and "Purple Heart Ridge." At Tanapag Harbor, in the northern part of the island, the Marines surrounded 4,000 Japanese soldiers. That was when the Japanese released their soldiers in a banzai attack in their final fight on the island.

Part of Japanese fighting strategies was to release a wave of soldiers onto the allies. The Japanese did this when they knew they were going to lose the battle and wanted to die with honors. But before dying on the battlefield, they wanted to harm as many allies as possible. It was usually done with knives, swords, grenades, and bayonets. Banzai attacks were notorious for their ferocity. This banzai attack was the largest one during the Pacific battles of World War II. The allies named these "banzai attacks" because the Japanese would shout "banzai" as they rushed the soldiers. In Japan, "banzai" means "long live his majesty, the Emperor."

On July 9, 1944, the day after the banzai attack, the Marines planted an American flag on Saipan in a show of victory. In the four days that followed, nearly 5,000 Japanese men, women, and children, who lived on the island, killed themselves by jumping off of a high cliff. It was later dubbed with the name "Suicide Cliff." There were still others that committed suicide with scythes (farmer's cropping tool), razor blades, ropes, rocks, and sticks. Japanese propaganda convinced them that if the American soldiers arrived, they would torture, rape, and murder them. In which case, suicide was their only means of escape. Americans shouted through loudspeakers, begging them to stop, but they refused to listen.

Ota Masahide, a survivor from the Battle of Saipan, described what was happening. "As the mayhem unfolded, they found all sorts of ways to kill... Men bashed their wives and parents bashed their children, young people killed the elderly, and the strong killed the weak," Masahide said. "What they felt in common was the belief that they were doing this out of love and compassion."

Japanese citizens felt let down because their Prime Minister, General Hideki Tojo made a promise, in public, that the United States would never take the island of Saipan. He was forced to resign a week after the Battle of Saipan ended.

Part 7

Battle of the Philippine Sea
June 19, 1944 - June 20, 1944

The Battle of the Philippine Sea was a naval battle between the Japanese Combined Fleet and the U.S. 5th Fleet. It took place amid the Battle of Saipan, while the U.S. Navy was protecting the waters outside of Saipan while the battle raged. It began on the morning of June 19th, when Admiral Jisaburo Ozawa sent 423 planes in 4 waves of attacks onto the American warships. That was a wrong decision on their behalf. He thought the U.S. Ships would have their guards down as they were maintaining the waters during the battle onshore. That was not the case. The American ships were under the watch of Admiral Raymond Spruance, and he was well prepared for an attack.

As the airplanes dropped bombs onto the warships, a pilot from the USS Lexington commented, "Why, hell, it was just like an old-time turkey shoot down home!" They then nicknamed that part of the battle the "Marianas Turkey Shoot." On the first day, the Japanese lost 395 planes though the United States lost only 20 aircraft. The next day the Japanese lost approximately 250 more, and the American troops lost more than 100 planes.

The Japanese retreated on June 20t, giving the victory to the Americans. In the two days that they fought, the Japanese fleet was decimated, having lost 315 of the planes they sent to attack us. Two of their aircraft carriers, Shokaku and Taiho, were sunk by torpedoes fired from the USS Cavalla and the USS Albacore. These were the largest aircraft-carrier fights in World War II. It was also the first time the Imperial Japanese Navy was not able to recover after a loss.

A debate stemming from the battle was Spruance's decision to lay back on the attacks on the second day when he saw that the Japanese would have no choice but to surrender. Many believe that had he fought just as hard. It further crippled the Japanese Imperial Navy to the point that the Battle of the Leyte Gulf may have never happened.

## Part 8

## Battle of Peleliu
### September 15, 1944 - November 27, 1944

The Battle of Peleliu began on September 15, 1944, just two days before the Battle of Angaur. The two islands were separated by a peninsula that was only 6 miles wide. The 1$^{st}$ Marine Division and the U.S. Army's 81$^{st}$ Infantry raided the island to gain control of an airstrip.

The Americans predicted that the battle would last only four days. They gained control of most of the island in the first week. It was the northern part of the island that would take two months to seize. The U.S. Navy set up a blockade to keep Japanese reinforcements and supplies from reaching the island. The Japanese troops dug in deep to their positions on the island and were not going to give up easily.

There were three types of caves on the island, natural limestone caves, artificial ones, and improved natural caves. Japanese forces inside the caves had enough supplies to last for 100 days. They used the caves for a variety of purposes, The "water cavities" formed by subterranean streams made flame thrower attacks ineffective. "Balcony caves" on the ridge slopes were prime spots for machine-gun nests and sniper positions. "Vertical fault caves," the largest of the caves, were often turned into command posts with electricity, communications facilities and living quarters for several soldiers. There were 500 caves altogether, and the allies attacked each and every one of them. They fired artillery directly into the caves. The flame throwers had a 150-yard-long spray of chemical fire that struck soldiers inside and outside the caves, no matter how well they were hidden. They also poured oil and gasoline into the downward sloping caves and then lit the trail on fire. Nearly 1,500 Japanese soldiers and 240 U.S. soldiers were killed in the final month of battle, trying to dislodge the Japanese from their caves. In one of the caves, a group of 49 Japanese soldiers refused to surrender, so the U.S. troops sealed the exits to the cave with cement.

On October 13, the Marines encircled the surviving Japanese soldiers. But still, fighting to the death, the Japanese would yet not surrender. The Battle did not end until November 27, 1944. The Marines lost approximately

1,800 soldiers, and nearly 8,000 more were wounded. That made up 40% of their troops. The National Museum of the Marine Corps, refer to it as "the bitterest battle of the war for the Marines." Of the Japanese soldiers that died in the Battle of Peleliu, many succumbed to starvation, thirst, suffocation, and concussions from blasts inside the caves.

Part 9

Battle of Angaur
September 17, 1944 - October 22, 1944

The small limestone island of Angaur sits just 3 miles in length among the Palau Islands. There were 1,400 Japanese soldiers stationed there on September 17, 1944, when American troops rolled onto the island to take control.

Admiral William Halsey, Jr. argued before the invasion that the operation was not essential and should not happen. Others believed that both the Battle of Angaur and the Battle of Peleliu were not necessary. It was also said that these battles were tying up resources for the troops and causing friction between the U.S. Marines and Army. That began when Marine Corps Lieutenant General Holland ("Howlin' Mad") Smith had relieved the Army's Major General Ralph Smith of his command of the 27th Infantry Division claiming 'defective performance.' However, General MacArthur deemed it important to gain control of the islands because the airfields put Japan in a position to take over the Philippines. MacArthur was preparing to embark in a battle to retake the Philippines.

The battle started on the eastern side of the island and advanced onto "the Bowl," a hill near Lake Salome. The Bowl was the toughest part of the battle. There were 750 Japanese soldiers defending it. By September 30th, the Japanese were weakened by hunger, thirst and artillery fire giving way for the Americans to take full control of the Bowl. It seemed then that the battle would be over. However, there were still a few hundred Japanese soldiers scattered about in clusters that did not want to give up.

U.S. troops used explosives, tanks, artillery, and flamethrowers to force the Japanese from the caves on the islands where a bulk of the resistance was coming from. After this, they used bulldozers to seal the entrances to the caves. Though the Americans lost more soldiers than the Japanese, they won possession of the island on October 22, 1944. By the end of the battle, 260

American soldiers killed and another 1354 were wounded. The Japanese lost 1338 soldiers, and another 59 were captured.

## Part 10

### Battle of Leyte Gulf
### October 23, 1944 - October 26, 1944

The Battle of the Leyte Gulf was fought in the waters of the Philippine islands near the islands of Leyte, Samar, and Luzon. It consisted of four separate engagements, each lasting one day. They were the Battle of the Sibuyan Sea (October 24), the Battle of Surigao Strait (October 25), the Battle of Samar (October 25), and the Battle of Cape Egano (October 25-26). The United States teamed with the Australian military, and they both wanted to isolate the Japanese from the Asian territories that they gained possession of previously. The Japanese needed a victory to regain a position of power.

The Allies had over 300 more ships than Japan. However, the Japanese had the advantage of land-based aircraft and their first kamikaze pilots. Multiple admirals led both the American and Japanese navies. Neither force had a unified command, which led to problems for both.

Though the Battle of Leyte Gulf lasted only four days, it was the largest Naval battle fought during World War II, with over 200,000 soldiers participating. The United States alone lost seven warships, while the Japanese lost twenty-six. The biggest defeat for the Japanese was the sinking of the Musashi. It was not an easy task. It took the allies 259 planes firing 19 torpedo and 17 bombs to sink the Musashi. It also crippled the Japanese Navy nearly annihilating them altogether. They were forced back to their base. They were unable to try and seize any more territory for the length of the war.

## Part 11

### Battle of Iwo Jima
### February 19, 1945 - March 26, 1945

One of the most significant battles fought in World War II was the Battle of Iwo Jima. On February 19, 1945, the U.S. Marine Corps and Navy teamed together to seize the island of Iwo Jima, located just 750 miles from the coast of Japan. It was occupied by the Imperial Japanese Army who had three airfields on the island. The Americans named this plan of attack "Operation

Detachment." They expected the battle to last only a few days, especially since the entire area is 8 square miles. They did not expect to see that the Japanese had a strategic plan of defense prepared, which included the ability to camouflage attack points among the dense trees. They were also surprised to learn that the beach they first landed on was not made of sand but thick volcanic ash. It was difficult to maneuver vehicles through it and did not provide safe footing. Some dunes were 15-feet high.

Before storming the island, they launched several warning attacks over a three-day period. When the response was weaker than they expected, they assumed that the Japanese no longer had a strong military stance on the island. They were wrong. That was all a part of the plan of Lieutenant General Tadamichi Kuribayashi, who was assigned the task of defending Iwo Jima.

Both sides were heavily equipped. The Japanese had a network of bunkers, hidden artillery positions and 11 miles of underground tunnels that connected 1,500 rooms, artillery emplacements, bunkers, ammunition dumps, and pillboxes. These tunnels also made it possible for Japanese soldiers to reoccupy barracks that the U.S. soldiers already attacked. The American soldiers had extensive naval artillery (projectile firing weapons mounted on ships) and dominated the airspace with Navy and marine airships. They were also armed with flame throwers that were used to attack Japanese troops in Japanese troops in pillboxes, caves, buildings, and bunkers. Each platoon had a soldier that was assigned to be the flame flower. The Americans also had an advantage in the size of troops. They had three times more than Japan.

Mount Suribachi was the highest point of the island and was the point of the heaviest fighting from the Japanese. There were several hidden tunnels carved into Mount Suribachi that U.S. soldiers passed by because they did not see them. However, the Japanese saw them and fired on them as they approached. After four days the Marines were able to take control of Mount Suribachi and cut it off from the rest of the island. The Marines were given a flag to hoist atop Mount Suribachi once they gained control over the area, and that is exactly what they did. Associated Press photographer, Joe Rosenthal, captured the iconic image of the flag being planted in victory. It was the first foreign flag to ever fly on Japanese land. Japanese forces were running low on food and supplies when they launched the final battle was fought on March 25, 1945. Kuribayashi led this attack by the Japanese soldiers. They surrendered the island to American soldiers the next day, March 26th. During the Battle of Iwo Jima, of the 21,000 Japanese soldiers that fought in the Battle of Iwo

Jima, approximately 300 survived. The Marines lost almost 7,000 soldiers. There were 22 U.S.

soldiers awarded the Medal of Honor. It is more than any other battle fought during World War II.

Due to the heavy fighting, the island was deemed worthless from all of the damage. United States Naval Construction Battalion (known as Seabees) was able to rebuild the landing strips so they could be used for emergency landings in the war. But their plans to build a fleet base, for the Navy, and a staging base for the Army, (where vehicles and aircraft could be assembled), was no longer an option.

The United States retained control of Iwo Jima until 1968 when they returned it to Japan. They established a Naval Air Base on the island, and to this day they allow the American military to share the base with them.

Part 12

Battle of Okinawa
April 1, 1945 - June 22, 1945

When the Allies first set out to attack Okinawa, they had two objectives in mind. First, they wanted to eliminate the remaining Japanese Navy. Second, they wanted to seize control of the island's four airfields. The first American troops, soldiers of the 77th Infantry Division, arrived on March 26th. Unfortunately, they misjudged the location and missed their mark. Instead of Okinawa, they embarked on the Kerama Islands which is 15 miles west of Okinawa. They reached Okinawa six days later. That is officially when the Battle of Okinawa began – Easter Sunday, April 1, 1945.

The next mistake of the allies was to underestimate the number of Japanese soldiers on the island. They thought there were approximately 64,000 soldiers and civilians. They instantly found themselves swarmed by 110,000 Japanese soldiers on the land, in the air, and the sea.

The Battle was called the "typhoon of steel" due to the intensity and brutal the fighting that took place. The Japanese unleashed a series of kamikaze attacks. The kamikazes were a part of the Japanese Special Attacks Units of military invaders who made deliberate suicidal crashes into enemy targets. The main reason the Japanese fought so hard was that Okinawa was the last obstacle in reaching Japan, itself. When the Japanese commander-in-chief on

Okinawa, Lieutenant-General Mitsuru Ushijima, committed ritual suicide on June 22$^{nd}$, the Japanese surrendered the island.

Several battles in the Pacific claim to be the largest amphibious battle of the Pacific, but it is the Battle of Okinawa that genuinely earned that title. The Japanese forces suffered lost over 110,000 soldiers. There were other civilian deaths, many of which committed suicide, and another 100,000 civilian casualties. They had 7,400 soldiers captured as Prisoners of War. Sixteen of their ships sunk and they lost 7,800 airplanes. The most significant loss was when their warship Yamato was destroyed in the battle. The Americans lost 12,000 soldiers, and another 38,000 were wounded. Among their artillery, 36 ships were sunk, 368 were damaged, and they lost 763 aircraft. The Battle of Okinawa, also known as Operation Iceberg, was the last major battle of World War II.

***There were quite a few battles fought in the Pacific during World War II. Not all of them directly involved the American military forces. The Battles mentioned are just some of the fights the soldiers endured. Every American – man and woman – who put on a military uniform during World War II, to serve our country, will forever be a hero in the eyes of the world!***

During World War II, Japan was successful in seizing control of Kiska one of the Aleutian Islands off Alaska. But that would not last for long. On August 15, 1953, nearly 35,000 United States and Canadian troops stormed the island to take back control. What they did not know was that Japan was warned that they were coming and had already abandoned the island. Somehow, 21 soldiers were still killed from friendly fire and booby traps.

Calvin Graham was 12-years-old when he lied about his age so that he could enlist in the Navy. He also forged his mother's signature and notary stamp, dressed in his older brother's clothes, and disguised his voice to make it deeper. He was sworn in on August 15, 1942. Several months later, he was serving aboard the South Dakota when the ship was attacked. It was then that Graham was injured in battle. His mother saw him on the news as they discussed the attack on the USS South Dakota. She contacted the military and revealed his true age. He was awarded the Bronze Star Medal and the Purple Heart Medal. Unfortunately, he was then dishonorably discharged in April 1943 for lying to the military about his age. Years later, an Act of

Congress reversed his status to an honorable discharge. They also restored the military benefits that were due to him.

Several celebrities were serving in the war who wanted to be on the frontline. The military denied their requests for fear that their celebrity status would make them prime targets for a kidnapping. That would put the rest of the platoon in even more danger. Being detained as an American Prisoner of War was pretty grueling, based on who was holding you captive. The POW camps in Japan were worse than the ones in Germany. Approximately 80,000 American soldiers were held in POW camps throughout the war. By the end, 27,000 were killed.

Prisoners of the war were treated so well in America that they returned years after for a reunion with fellow prisoners. But as it always is with the American government, the citizens were not treated anywhere nearly as good. They endured several rations. This was due to the bulk of the items in America were being used in the war. There were rations on clothing, rubber, metal, and food. It was difficult for farmers to transport fresh food due to rations on gasoline and tires. It was a higher priority to transport soldiers and supplies than it was to carry food, especially coffee and sugar. Even so, some items were also rationed to the soldiers. In fact, American soldiers received a ration of 22 toilet paper squares a day. The United States government's Office of Price Administration's solution to making sure families received their fair share was to issue ration stamps. Every American family was given ration books and could use the stamps to purchase household goods and many types of food such as meat, sugar, coffee, tea, jam, biscuits, breakfast cereals, cheese, cooking oil, milk, eggs, chocolate, bacon, canned food, and butter. Fresh fruits and vegetables were not part of the ration program but were in short supply. Nutella was invented during the war because of the rations. There was a shortage of chocolate, so Italian Pastry Maker, Pietro Ferrero, mixed hazelnuts into his cocoa to extend his chocolate supply.

When families received their ration books, each stamp was designated to a specific item. And that product could only be purchased with a ration stamp. Families would receive new books every month. The program started on January 8, 1940 and soon after 8,000 boards were erected across the country to run the group.

*Reflections Part I*

It was America's decision to drop the atomic bomb on Japan that forced them into surrendering. The first bomb was dropped on Hiroshima on August 6th; the second was on Nagasaki on August 9th. They planned to drop a third bomb on Tokyo but reconsidered since Japan announced that they were surrendering.

Throughout the war, Hitler hoped to get his hands on the atomic bomb. So much so, that he tried to have Danish nuclear physicist Niels Bohr kidnapped. Hitler knew that Bohr studied atomic structure. He even won a Nobel Prize in Physics for it in 1922. He wanted Bohr to construct an atomic bomb for him. When the Germans invaded Denmark, Bohr fled from his house while resistance fighters held off the soldiers. Bohr only stopped to pick up a beer bottle full of 'heavy water.'

Two dates are disputed on as being the final day of World War II. The first date is August 15, 1945, the day Japan announced its plans to surrender. The second day is September 2, 1945, the day Japan signed the documents to surrender. That came to be known as Victory Over Japan Day – or V-J Day. Even though World War II has ended, Russia and Japan have yet to sign the Peace Treaty.

*An aerial view of Pearl Harbor, December 1940.*

*Joe George was posthumously awarded a Bronze Star with a "V" device for valor for saving the last six sailors on board the USS Arizona, during the attack on Pearl Harbor.*

*Alexander Vracui shot down six Japanese planes during one mission, the Great Marianas Turkey Shoot.*

*A Grumman Hellcat crash landing on the USS Enterprise, the greatest Naval Vessel of WW II.*

*Reflections Part I*

*The USS Lexington, a U.S. aircraft carrier, was lost during the 1942 Battle of the Coral Sea.*

*Torpedo bombers en route to the Battle of the Philippine Sea.*

*The memorial rock on Wake Island that is named "The 98 Rock." It is a tribute to the lives lost there.*

*American soldiers celebrating their victory at the Battle of Iwo Jima.*

*Despite being outnumbered in the battle of Midway, the Americans were victorious.*

*Emperor Hirohito and his staff aboard Musashi on June 24, 1943. The Musashi battleship was built in secrecy. Even it's launching was only attended by a few military personnel.*

## Reflections Part I

Offloading tanks at Guadalcanal.

Lieutenant McClusky's two small squadrons launched from Enterprise the morning of June 4, 1942.

In the Battle of Midway, the United States lost one carrier, one destroyer, and 150 aircraft.

*One of the last photos of Yamato, on fire and listing just before the massive explosion.*

*Smoke ascended more than 20,000 feet when Yamato exploded.*

*The Yamato and Musashi at the Truk Islands.*

*Tony K. Burris of Blanchard, Oklahoma received the Silver Star and the Medal of Honor for his actions in the Korean War.*

*Tony Burris Memorial in Blanchard, Oklahoma.*

## Part 13

## The Korean War

In July of 1950 Tony K. Burris of Blanchard, Oklahoma enlisted in the U.S. Army. Tony was 20 years old. During his time in the Army Tony wrote more than 60 letters to family and friends. July 30, 1950 Tony wrote in his first letter, "Most of the guys in my barracks are seventeen or eighteen years old. They sort of look up to me". Tony's last letter was written October 4,1951. In the letter he wrote "If the rotation plans aren't changed, I may get out of here somewhere around the first of December". Tony was killed on Heartbreak Ridge October 9,1951. the country was still reshaping itself from the effects of World War II. There was a mixture of changes from the war. The greatest one is that selling weapons to foreign countries during the war helped to pull America from the Great Depression, which started when Wall Street collapsed on October 29, 1929. America began to flourish once again.

However, a few short years later, Americans found themselves at war again, this time with Korea. Before the end of World War II, Korea was one country. But the close of World War II started the arms race between the Soviet Union and America, each country battling to be the powerhouse of weaponry. This caused tensions with other countries, one of them being Korea. There was already tension between North and South Korea. That seemed to push an already existent rift to deepen, thanks to the meddling of the Soviet Union.

North Korea claimed the status of a socialist state, under the leadership of communist Kim Il-sung; whereas South Korea took the stance as a capitalist state under the leadership of anti-communist Syngman Rhee. Though there was a border at the 38$^{th}$ parallel, each half claimed to be the actual governing party of Korea and refused to recognize the border. It boiled over on June 25, 1950, at 4:30 am, when 75,000 North Korean soldiers, accompanied by the Soviet Union and China, crossed the 38$^{th}$ parallel and invaded South Korea. The result was 21 countries coming to the aide of South Korea with America leading the pack. In fact, 90% of the soldiers fighting for South Korea were from America.

The Battle of Pork Chop Hill stands out because the winner is dependant on who you ask. It was a fight that was made of two battles. It all began when the Chinese attacked Old Baldy, an outpost near Pork Chop Hill, and were able to gain control of the area. The Americans counterattacked the next day, on April 16, 1953, and were able to take it back when the Chinese retreated on April 18th.

The Chinese were not about to let it go for long. They came back on July 6th and attacked the hill again. This time it would be the Chinese that forced the Americans to concede the hill on July 11th.

The U.S. lost 243 soldiers. The Chinese had a loss of approximately 1,500 soldiers. The fight to gain possession of the hill was longer than any other single battlefield in Korea. The site of the battle was titled Hill 255, but the contour lines it made on a map gave it an unusual design that later earned it the name – Pork Chop Hill.

The war raged on until July 27, 1953, when the Korean Armistice Agreement was signed. American soldiers were coming home, and prisoners of war were being released from both halves of Korea. With the agreement came the Korean Demilitarized Zone. This is an area of land that stretches across the Korean Peninsula. It serves as a buffer between the North and South. Neither side of Korea ever signed a Peace Treaty, so the war between them has never come to an end. It is simply frozen in an unofficial peace.

Each of the leading country's involvement in the war referred to it by a different name. North Korea called it the "625," marking the date of June 25h. South Korea related to it as the "Fatherland Liberation War." The Soviet Union labeled it the "War to Resist America and Aid Korea." In America, President Harry Truman referred to it as a "Police State" since he never officially declared war. His actions were a response to South Korea's cry for help. The American people called it the "Forgotten War" because the dedication and loss to the soldiers were never fully acknowledged by the government or the people. We seem to have "forgotten" that there are still more than 7,000 U.S. soldiers missing in action.

*February 11, 1954: Marilyn Monroe entertaining thousands of US Troops in Korea.*

Part 14

The Vietnam War

The start of the Vietnam War was similar to the Korean War, in the way that it was the North versus the South. It began with the desire of North Vietnam to make their entire country a Communist regime. South Vietnam wanted a government closer to the Democracy that America had. With the assistance of China, the North declared war on the South on November 1, 1955. As the war between the two halves continued through the years, the United States grew worried. They thought if the North would win in their attempts to turn the South into a communist territory that communism could spread throughout the rest of Asia. This idea was known as the "Domino Effect." That was the chief concern of President Nixon and why he chose to bring the United States into the Vietnam War, on the side of the South, on March 8, 1965.

## Reflections Part I

The North Vietnamese (communists) had a few countries fighting on their side. Those included the Viet Cong, the People's Republic of China and the Soviet Union. South Vietnam (anti-communist) had the United States of America, South Korea, Australia, New Zealand, Thailand, and Laos all fighting on their side during the war.

During the Vietnam War, soldiers found creative ways to use everyday objects. One of them was the slinky. The soldiers used them as mobile radio antennas by throwing them over branches to extend the range of their radios. Superglue was used during the Vietnam War to slow the bleeding of wounded soldiers until they could get to a hospital. And duct tape was used to fix helicopter wings.

They also had to find more creative ways to battle with the North Vietnamese soldiers, a sort of mental warfare. They replaced the ammunition used by the Viet Cong with explosive decoy ammunition, which destroyed their weapons when fired.

An Air Force Sergeant created an "underground" radio station, (in the back of a Vietnamese brothel) and would play hard rock, make vulgar jokes and openly oppose the war. He even operated his radio shows on channel 69.

The Vietnamese believed that if people did not receive a proper burial when they died that their angry spirit would wander the Earth forever. So, to play on this fear, American soldiers made recordings of ghost voices and spooky sounds. They played them at night on speakers that they had hidden in the jingle. It led Vietnamese soldiers to believe that the souls of dead soldiers were wandering outside.

The soldiers were told that the Vietnamese were superstitious and also believed that the Ace of Spades card was a symbol of death. Upon seeing the card, they would run away. When the U.S. Playing Card Company learned of this, they shipped crates of this card to Vietnam. American soldiers would scatter them during raids and leave them on the bodies of the fallen soldiers to scare the Vietnamese. The cards were also stuck on items belonging to the U.S. soldiers. It turned out the information about the car was not true – at first. By the end of the war, the Vietnamese honestly did believe that the card was a symbol of death.

Meanwhile, in the United States, citizens were in a bitter rivalry with each other. It started with a stream of protests against a war that they felt we should not be involved in, and later towards a draft that they believed to be unfair. Protesters even requested a permit to levitate the Pentagon 300 feet in the air, through songs and chants, to exorcise it of its evil and end the Vietnam War. The Pentagon jokingly agreed but said they only give consent to three feet. Soon they turned their anger onto soldiers who were returning home from Vietnam. When the protests started, many believe that the press fueled the flames to that fire and even reported fake news to keep the protesters angry. These protests often turned violent. Screenwriter Terry Gilliam was at a Vietnam War protest and witnessed just how violent it could escalate. He stated, "I got my head bashed in at a demonstration against the Vietnam War. Police were losing control because they were up against a world they really didn't understand." It is understandable to be angry with the government over a war that some were against. But it was not fair in any way to direct that anger onto the soldiers. Many of them also did not agree with the war but were forced to be there because of the draft. However, the barrage of negative reports by the media continued to sour their public's views of the war – and the soldiers.

The way the draft worked is that 366 plastic balls were dumped into a large glass container. Each one had a month and date written on it. The very first one chosen was September 14$^{th}$. That meant that everyone born on that day between 1944-1950 was called into duty. After they made that selection, they performed a second draft. With this one, the capsules held the 26 letters of the alphabet. The letter chosen would reflect the order the men would be called in. They would start with that letter and then work alphabetically. During the Vietnam War, they utilized the draft 195 times. That resulted in 2,200,000 solders being drafted.

Many men were able to avoid the draft. Several exceptions made that possible. If your religion forbids you to participate in a war, this will exclude you. Those religions are Jehovah's Witnesses, Mennonites, the Amish, and Quakers. People belonging to those denominations could assist the soldiers in other ways but only as a civilian.

Ill health could make someone ineligible for the draft. Some conditions that will get you denied are anemia, flat feet, gastritis, ulcers, hepatitis, depression, and diabetes. Some people would go weeks without bathing and days without sleeping before their draft hearing to convince the military that they were mentally unstable. Ted Nugent is notorious for his actions. He went a month without bathing or brushing his hair. On his way to the draft hearing, he urinated and defecated in his pants.

## Reflections Part I

If you were a married man, with children, you could put off being drafted. The military would also not accept homosexuals. During the wars of the '50s and '60s, it was legal to ask and tell. Some men would wear lady's underwear on the day of their physical to convince the military that they were gay.

Two of the most common ways to avoid the draft were moving to Canada and enrolling in college. During the Vietnam War, approximately 40,000 men moved to Canada for that purpose. Being a college student did not completely rule you out from the draft. It would merely delay it by giving the student a deferment. President Donald Trump received for of them. Several former Presidents also received deferments. Bill Clinton received one, Joe Biden received five, and Dick Cheney also received five.

You could also avoid the draft if you had a job that was considered vital, and something that no one else could take over for you. Oklahoma native, Ron Howard, was starring on Happy Days at the time. He used this to avoid the draft. He explained to the military that he was the star of a TV series (which he was). If he were drafted, thousands of people would lose their jobs; jobs that they needed to support their families. They accepted that, and he was precluded from the draft. Some celebrities did not let their Hollywood status stop them from serving. Those celebrities are Clark Gable, Josephine Baker, and Jimmy Stewart. On January 27, 1973, President Nixon announced that he signed the Paris Peace Accords and that America was withdrawing from Vietnam. To date, this remains the longest fought war that the United States participated in. North Vietnam accepted a cease-fire in the days that the American soldiers were returning home. Approximately 2,700,000 American men and women served in the Vietnam War. More than 58,000 of those soldiers were killed, and another 304,000 were injured. Among them, 75,000 were disabled. Nearly 2,000 soldiers were held as Prisoners of War (POW).

For the first time, the American government and a majority of the citizens failed to support the U.S. soldiers. They were spat on by their fellow countrymen when they got off the airplanes, returning from war. The soldiers were also sometimes attacked in the streets of America. This pales in comparison to the psychological effects that the war had on those men and women. Whether you agree with America's participation or not, there is one thing we can all agree on about it. The men and women who served in that war are every bit as honorable as the soldiers who served in every single war before and after that. May we never forget their sacrifice.

Since the day the Paris Peace Accords was signed, there has been a debate on whether or not America won the Vietnam War. Nixon explained it best when he said, "No event in American history is more misunderstood than the Vietnam War. It was misreported then, and it is misremembered now." If you want to know the truth, you will find the answer from the ones directly involved at the time. Bruce Herschensohn, of Pepperdine University School of Public Policy, explained just what happened. The truth that so many have tried to cover up.

*Decades back, in late 1972, South Vietnam and the United States were winning the Vietnam War decisively by every conceivable measure. That's not just my view. That was the view of our enemy, the North Vietnamese government officials. The victory was apparent when President Nixon ordered the U.S. Air Force to bomb industrial and military targets in Hanoi. It was North Vietnam's capital city, and in Haiphong, its major port city. Nixon stated we would stop the bombing if the North Vietnamese would attend the Paris Peace Talks that they had left earlier. The North Vietnamese did go back to the Paris Peace talks, and we did stop the bombing as promised.*

*On January 23rd, 1973, President Nixon gave a speech to the nation on primetime television. He announced that the Paris Peace Accords that had been initialed by the United States, South Vietnam, North Vietnam, the Viet Cong, and the Accords would be signed on the 27th.*

*What the United States and South Vietnam received in those accords was a victory. At the White House, it was called "VV Day," "Victory in Vietnam Day."*

*The U.S. backed up that victory with a simple pledge within the Paris Peace Accords saying: should the South require any military hardware to defend itself against any North Vietnam aggression we would provide replacement aid to the South on a piece-by-piece, one-to-one replacement, meaning a bullet for a bullet; a helicopter for a helicopter, for all things lost — replacement. Those accords had halted the advance of communist tyranny.*

*Then it all came apart. And It happened this way: In August of the following year, 1974, President Nixon resigned his office as a result of what became known as "Watergate." Three months after his resignation was the November congressional elections. The Democrats won a landslide victory for the new Congress. Many of the members used their new majority to defund the military aid the U.S. had promised. Piece-by-piece they broke the commitment that we made to the South Vietnamese*

## Reflections Part I

in Paris to provide whatever military hardware the South Vietnamese needed in case of aggression from the North. To put it simply, a majority of Democrats of the 94th Congress did not keep the word of the United States.

On April the 10th of 1975, President Gerald Ford appealed directly to those members of the congress in an evening Joint Session, televised to the nation. In that speech, he begged Congress to keep the word of the United States. But as President Ford delivered his speech, many of the members of Congress walked out of the chamber. They had an investment in America's failure in Vietnam. They also participated in demonstrations against the war for many years. They would not give the aid that was promised.

On April 30th, South Vietnam surrendered, and Re-education Camps were constructed, bringing on the phenomenon of the Boat People began. If the South Vietnamese had received the arms that the United States promised them, would the result have been different? It already had been changed. The North Vietnamese leaders admitted that they were testing the new President, Gerald Ford. They took one village after another, then cities, then provinces, and our only response was to go back on our word. The U.S. did not re-supply the South Vietnamese as we had promised. It was then that the North Vietnamese knew they were on the road to South Vietnam's capital city, Saigon. Soon after, it was renamed Ho Chi Minh City.

Former Arkansas Senator William Fulbright, who had been the Chairman of the Senate Foreign Relations Committee made a public statement about the surrender of South Vietnam. He said this, "I am no more distressed than I would be about Arkansas losing a football game to Texas." The U.S. knew that North Vietnam would violate the accords and so we planned for it. What we did not know was that our own Congress would violate the agreements. And break them, of all things, on behalf of the North Vietnamese. That's what happened.

~ Bruce Herschensohn (A Political Commentator who worked in the Nixon administration, primarily as a speechwriter. He was also a part of the Reagan Administration. He later taught politics at the University of Maryland, Whittier College, and Pepperdine University.)

*Soldiers filling their canisters with rainwater as it cascades off the leaves.*

## Reflections Part I

*Jimi Hendrix playing guitar during his time in the United States Army, 1961*

*This soldier wore cards on his helmet to remind him of his parents – his king and queen.*

*A U.S soldier keeping the children safe.*

*A member of the 3rd Marines decorated both his helmet and his flack jacket.*

## Did you know?

- *Just before midnight on July 19-20, 1952 a UFO was spotted on radar and by witnesses on the ground in Washington, D.C. This incident started the UFO phenomenon that would continue for decades. UFO toys, movies, and TV shows also became popular.*

- *After World War II, America tried to buy Greenland for $100,000,000. Denmark declined.*

- *The shortest war in history was between Zanzibar and England in 1896. Zanzibar surrendered after 40 minutes.*

- *During World War II Americans referred to "hamburgers" as "Liberty steak." They did that because the word "hamburger" sounded too German.*

- *Two Japanese soldiers stayed hidden in the caves on the island of Iwo Jima and did not surrender until four years after World War II ended.*

There is always that one soldier

Lowell Williams in Vietnam, 1968. Lowell was one of my closest friends.

*Reflections Part I*

*A tintype photo of Jesse James (right) seated beside his one-time partner and eventual killer Robert Ford (left)*

*A Wanted Poster of Frank and Jesse James through the years of their criminal activity*

# Chapter 7

# Harmans Move West

When the Harmans decided to leave Kentucky and move west, they each had their own ideas of where they hoped to settle. But life had other plans for some of them. Pain had taken over Peter's body from years of back-breaking work on the farm, and his health was failing. That was the principal reason for the move. Peter and Mary set out for Rock, Kansas to live near their son, KC. He and his wife, Ellen, moved there a few years prior. When KC learned of his father's health issues, he asked his parents to move closer to them in case they needed any help. KC and Ellen wanted to be there for them.

Doc wanted to make the move with them. During the transition westward, they made a stop at Gallatin, Missouri, for a break. These breaks could last several weeks or several months, depending on the weather conditions. While they were there, Doc fell in love with Ella Frances Gilliland. He decided to stay so that he could marry Ella and they could start a life together. The couple married on September 29, 1879. A few days after the wedding, Mary and Peter set out once more for Rock, Kansas. It was all too much for Peter. He died on his 56$^{th}$ birthday, just hours before they reached Rock.

Through the years, both sides of Kenny's families (Harmans/Harmons and Perrins) endured some of life's most difficult struggles including droughts, tornadoes, floods, death of children, fatal accidents, illness, the Depression, and the Dust Bowl. He had family that served in battle from the days of the Civil War to the Vietnam War.

The Harmons even participated in the history-making Oklahoma Land Rush of 1889. No matter what life threw at the Harmons, they survived – as a family. They also had the fun of challenging each other. When they lived in Kansas, two of Curns' cousins, Cleve Portwood and Fleet Ewing, did this very thing over a steak. They were in the basement of a saloon and had been drinking for a while. They were both pretty tipsy when Portwood boldly claimed that he could eat a one-pound steak in just ONE BITE! The challenge was on – a wager was made – and a short time later, two men were dragging Portwood, by his feet, up the stairs trying to save his life. Portwood did survive.

Still, there was one family mystery that they were never able to solve. One of the biggest mysteries in the Harmon family revolved around Curns Sr. and the time he disappeared for eight months when they were living in Liberty, Missouri. Without any notice, he just left. No one heard from him, saw him, or even received a postcard stating where he was and what he was doing. One day Curns walked in the door like it was just later that afternoon from the day he vanished. He got something to eat, carried on a conversation about the day, and then walked out to go back to his farm work. It was like no time had gone by at all. He lived for 50 years more but never answered any questions about what went on during those eight months that he was gone.

Many family members believed he was with the Jesse James gang during those months. The childhood home of Frank and Jesse James was in Kearney, Missouri, which is in the area of Liberty and Gallatin, where Curns and his family lived. Frank and Jesse's father was a Baptist minister who left the family in 1840, for California, so that he could preach to the coal miners. Jesse picked up where his father left off and was outwardly religious. Many believed that like his father, he would also be a Minister one day. The Civil War changed that path for him. When Union soldiers raided his farm, torturing Jesse, his mother, and his stepfather, Reuben Samuel. They would hang Reuben from a rope strung up on a tall tree branch only to let him down when he was close to death. They did this repeatedly before finally leaving. Jesse's life changed completely after that day. He joined his brother who was fighting in a group of Guerrillas on the side of the Confederates. After the war, many of them took to robbing banks, and Jesse soon followed. His crime spree spread across ten states, the majority of it happening in Missouri.

The James family also had a strong connection to Oklahoma. In 1863, the brothers often stayed at Broken Arrow, Oklahoma, when it was Indian Territory. In the mid-1800s, before Oklahoma became a state, great cattle drives were traveling between Kansas and Texas, carving out ruts that would soon become roads. At the time, Oklahoma had vast open territories and only a few US Marshals to oversee things going on. It was known as the last untamed frontier. The James gang used Oklahoma as a safe haven when they were running from the law. Four areas, in particular, were most used by Jesse James and his gang. One was Younger's Bend (in Muskogee) where they could fill their canteens and water their horses. There was Horse Thief Spring (in Tulsa) which was a favorite stomping grounds. Then there was Robber's Cave (in Wilburton) that was filled with a structure of mazes, making it easy to escape the Marshals who were unfamiliar with the area. The last was Sugarloaf Mountain (in LeFlore County) that had a hotel which was a haven for outlaws.

During their escapes from the law, the James brothers often buried cash and gold. They meant to come back for it later. In some cases, they did, but they did not retrieve it all. After Jesse was killed in 1875, Frank turned himself in since he was still a "wanted man." Most charges were dropped for lack of evidence, and in 1905 he decided to retire to a life of farming, choosing Muskogee Oklahoma as his permanent home. At the time, Muskogee was only seven years old. He also owned a farm in Fletcher. He stayed there off-and-on from 1906-1911. His mother, Zerelda Samuel, died on board the Frisco train, leaving Oklahoma for California. She had just visited Frank at his home in Fletcher. They believe her death was caused from heart failure.

Frank later went back to each location where they buried money but could not find any of it. The land had changed so much. New homes and businesses were built over what was once Native American hunting ground. A railroad was built in locations that held markers leading to the places of the buried treasure. And the banks of the Poteau River, where they also buried loot, had been taken over by the deep river waters, swallowing up any treasure that was once buried there.

To this day, it is believed that a great deal of gold is still buried throughout Oklahoma, left behind by the James/Younger Gang. Some say that Jesse James hid 2 million dollars near Fort Sill, another $88,000 in what is now Chandler Park, and another $110,000 in a pit known as Robbers Canyon, near Pryor, Oklahoma.

The family may not have been too far off to believe that Curns was involved with Jesse James, during his absence. It was common for townspeople to befriend Jesse and Frank. And then there was the fact that later Curns son, Cecil, married Edith Cobb. Her mother had the last name, Younger. The

## Reflections Part I

Younger family is part of the group that rode with - the James/Younger Gang, named for Jesse and his brother Frank, and their partners in crime, brothers, Bob, Cole, and Jim Younger.

In 1877, two years after Jesse James died, Curns left Williamsburg, Kentucky for Liberty Missouri. He decided to move closer to his cousins. Twelve years later, in 1889, the families of KC, Uhel, Curns, and their sister, Liz, decided to move to Verden, Oklahoma. The families lived and farmed in Verden for about 15 years. They farmed numerous types of crops. However, three were notable. Those were the watermelons, cantaloupes, and sweet potatoes. urns quickly earned the nickname, "Tator" because his favorite crop was sweet potatoes. Together, Curns, Babe, Cecil, Bill, and Kenny raised melons for more than 80 years! During those years in Verde, some of the Harmans changed the spelling of their name – switching the 'A' to an 'O.' They went from Harman to Harmon. In the early 1900's the Harmans moved north to the Guthrie/Cashion Oklahoma area; while the Harmons moved east to the Dibble/Blanchard, Oklahoma Area.

As Oklahoma entered the nifty 50's, life-changing events unfolded all around them. The biggest was that the country added two new states – Alaska and Hawaii. The United States first bought Alaska from Russia on March 30, 1867, for 7.2 million dollars. That averaged out to about 2 cents an acre. Before Hawaii became a state, they held a special election asking the residents if they wanted to become a part of the United States. It was in their hands, and 93% of the people voted YES.

It was just before midnight on July 19, 1952, when a UFO was allegedly spotted on radar and by witnesses on the ground in Washington, DC. The incident started the UFO phenomenon that would continue for decades. A craze that would result in toys, movies, and TV shows. The "space race" between America and the USSR began in 1957, and a year later, the United States established NASA. This "new" space program had their first big success in 1961 when Alan Shepard piloted the Freedom 7 Capsule becoming the first American in space. Ten years after NASA began, Apollo 8 and its three-astronaut crew orbited the moon taking the "Earthrise" photograph. This image became world-famous. The world then watched nervously on July 20, 1969, as Neil Armstrong took the first steps out of Apollo 11, after it landed on the moon, uttering the now-famous words, "One small step for a man. One giant leap for mankind."

*The "Earthrise" photograph taken from lunar orbit by astronaut William Anders on December 24, 1968, during the Apollo 8 mission.*

A few historic changes included "In God We Trust" was first added to the dollar bill in 1956. That was decided after President Dwight Eisenhower adopted those words as the country's motto. Americans watched England crown a new queen, Elizabeth II, following the death of her father, King George VI, on February 6, 1952. Eleven years later, we lost our country's leader when John Kennedy (JFK) was shot on November 22, 1963, while riding in a motorcade. Bullets struck Kennedy in the neck and head. The car immediately sped off towards Parkland Memorial Hospital, but there was not anything they could do to save Kennedy. He died a half-hour after he was shot. The police arrested Lee Harvey Oswald for the shooting. A cloud of mystery continues to surround the events of that day. Many believe that the wrong man was arrested.

A rush of changes were stirring up inside the home. The first telephone answering machine, the Electronic Secretary, was released in 1957 and cost almost $200. Several people attempted the answering machine but fell short of what would work in the home. AT&T inventors created an answering machine in the early '30s, but they kept it secret because they believed that if families had the answering machine, they would not make as many phone calls. By 1950, homes also had the "lazy bones" the first TV remote control created by Zenith. It was a handheld device that plugged into the TV. Five years later, the Zenith engineer, Eugene Polley, came through for them with the first wireless TV remote control, the Flashmatic. It only had one button and was used to turn the TV on and off.

As if the TV was not significant enough, Swanson changed our world when they introduced the first TV dinner in 1953. It was a Thanksgiving-style dinner and consisted of turkey, cornbread dressing, peas, and sweet potatoes. It cost 98 cents and came in a box that resembled a TV. The first batch consisted of 5,000 dinners that were put together by hand by two dozen women. They were such a huge success that they ended up selling more than 10 million during the first year of production.

Loads of inventions were still on the way! J.D. Salinger published the Catcher in the Rye in 1951, which many believed was the cause of teens rebelling against their parents. Families were getting their first try at Super Glue, Benadryl, velcro, color TV, Con-Tact paper, instant iced tea (White Rose Redi-tea), colored kitchen appliances, and even Saran Wrap. Bubble wrap was introduced in 1957. It was created by accident when Alfred Fielding and Marc Chavannes were attempting to create a 3-D plastic wallpaper, not a packing material. The first credit card (Diner's Club) was introduced in 1958. For the children, there was the introduction of Mr. Potato Head, the first video game (Spacewar), Easy-Bake ovens, hula hoops, Charlie Brown, and Snoopy.

On October 25, 1955, the Raytheon Corporation introduced the first microwave for commercial use. It was called the Radarange. The name came from a company-wide contest. It cost $2,000. That would be more than $19,147 today! The first microwave sold for the home would not come until 1967. Amana (a division of Raytheon) created the microwave and sold it for $1,300. That would be more than $12,445 today! The first hard disc for a computer was made in 1955. It held 10 MB and cost $3,998. Today that would be $38,275.

Alabama Senator Rankin Fite made the first 911 call on February 16, 1968, in Haleyville, Alabama. The American Telephone and Telegraph Company (AT&T) derived the 911 system after meeting with the FCC over how they can develop a universal emergency number that could be used quickly. A year after their meeting, they chose to use the numbers 911. Why? Well, it is because it was quick, easy to remember, and it was the only three digits that had not been previously used as an office code or area code.

In 1963, zip codes were being used for the first time. By the way, "zip" stands for "zoning improvement plan." Cans now had pull tabs, and the smiley face was becoming an iconic symbol. It was first used in an ad to show the merger of two insurance companies. Two years later, smoke detectors were being installed in homes. They were initially introduced in the '40s, but they were too expensive for families to afford them.

There were many remarkable inventions and monumental moments that Kenny was lucky to see from the start. From all of the new items to emerge between 1950-1969, the greatest invention of all was the Polio vaccine by Jonas Salk on March 26, 1953.

Bell's Amusement Park in Tulsa opened in 1951. The Golden Driller unveiled in 1952. It is a 75-foot statue of an oil worker. It continues to be the 6th tallest statue in America. The first mall in Oklahoma opened its doors on October 8, 1956. The Penn Square Mall still stands today. They also saw the building of their first Daylight Donuts, in 1954 and the QuikTrip in 1958.

As the '60s rolled in, Kenny Harmon was turning ten years old. The years went by fast, and in no time, he was entering his teen years. As a teenager, there were many more changes for Kenny to experience. The Beatles were taking the music world by storm, America was embroiled in the Vietnam War, and the culture of hippies was growing.

Kenny became a fan of rock n' roll in the '50s when he was visiting his cousin, Glen Moore, in Pauls Valley. They listened to a stack of 45' rpm records on Glen's record player. That was the first time Kenny heard Elvis Presley. The song was "Hound Dog."

During the fall of '66, Kenny was cruising in his '57 Chevy, and he picked up his friend, Bobby Gray. The two always had fun just driving around, talking and listening to rock n' roll on the radio. Suddenly Bobby shouted, "Listen to that!" as he reached for the dial to turn up the volume. The song playing was "Devil With The Blue Dress On," a great song by a great band. By the end of the song, Kenny had found his new favorite band - Mitch Ryder and the Detroit Wheels. The following year, Kenny found Mitch Ryder's "Breakout" album in cousin Glen Moore's collection.

The music of Mitch Ryder and the Detroit Wheels radiated with Kenny, and to this day they are still his favorite band. One of the things he loved was how Mitch Ryder would add words that were not in the lyrics. Such as, at the end of "Devil with the Blue Dress On," as the music begins to fade, you hear Ryder yell, "Ah, sock it to me." Those very words were the title of the song they released next. So, in a way, they became the only band to introduce their next release at the end of a song.

Mitch Ryder coined the phrase "Sock it to me" before Aretha Franklin punched out those powerful words in her song, Respect. Soon, Laugh-in had their own "Sock it to Me" girl. She was Judy Carne (Burt Reynolds's first wife). However, Mitch Ryder never received credit for creating the "Sock it to me" line in music.

Devil with the Blue Dress On was the biggest hit for Mitch Ryder and the Detroit Wheels. It reached #4 on the charts and stayed there for more than six weeks. Bruce Springsteen said that Mitch Ryder had a considerable influence on his career.

Kenny had long been a sports buff of football and baseball. He was a dedicated fan of OU (University of Oklahoma) football. His first memory of OU games was of the Orange Bowl, played on January 1, 1958, between Oklahoma Sooners and Duke Blue Devils. It was the second Orange Bowl game for the Dukes and the fourth for the Sooners. The Sooners were outgained in yards and had more penalties, but that did not stop them from winning the championship game, 48-21. They had just started televising their games a few years prior on November 8, 1952, on NBC. It was OU against Notre Dame.

The first NFL game that Kenny watched was the championship game played between the Baltimore Colts and the New York Giants on December 28, 1958. It was the first NFL playoff game to go into sudden-death overtime and is referred to as the "Greatest Game Ever Played."

As for baseball, his favorite player was Mickey Mantle. He first listened to a game of Mantle and the Yankees in 1958. He was peddling melons and listening to the game as it played over the radio.

## High School Sweethearts

Kenny and Pat Roberts were classmates for 12 years. For the most part, they were just casual friends. She was a quiet girl and never seemed interested in him. That changed in the spring of 67' when they were in their junior year.

One afternoon Kenny was cruising in Dibble and pulled up to the Roberts family car. He noticed Pat waving enthusiastically from the back seat. He had never seen her so spirited. In class, she was more reserved. He waited a short time before approaching her for a date and was equally excited when she said YES! The summer of 67' belonged to Kenny and Pat. They dated exclusively, making many trips to the Hillcrest Drive-In Theater in Lindsay and the Chief Drive-In in Chickasha. In the fall, when the weather started getting colder, they switched to the Washita Theater in Chickasha.

Kenny and Pat dated for over a year. They said good-bye in June 1968. She was the only girl to wear his class ring. Because he was difficult to understand and tolerate, she returned the ring twice to him before the final time. Pat will always hold a place in his heart. To this day, they are still friends.

Reflections Part I

## *Did you know?*

- *The compact disc was invented in 1965. However, music fans preferred 8 track cassettes. So, it sat in the patent office until its re-release in 1981.*

- *Jesse James' father was a Baptist Minister and a Hemp farmer.*

- *Roll-on deodorant was invented in 1952. Before the invention of Ban Roll-On, the most common deodorant was Everdry, an aluminum chloride solution that was applied with cotton swabs. Besides being messy and taking forever to dry, Everdry also had the side effect of eating through clothes.*

- *In 1958, Bette Nesmith Graham invented "Mistake Out" later renamed, Liquid Paper. Bette was the mother of Mike Nesmith from the Monkees. She got the idea when she observed workers painting over a billboard with white paint so they can put up a new ad.*

- *Talk Show Host, Maury Povich was a gopher in the radio booth for the 1958 NFL championship between the Baltimore Colts and the New York Giants. He kept stats and ran errands for the future Hall of Fame broadcaster, Bob Wolff. At halftime, he even read a few first-half numbers on the air.*

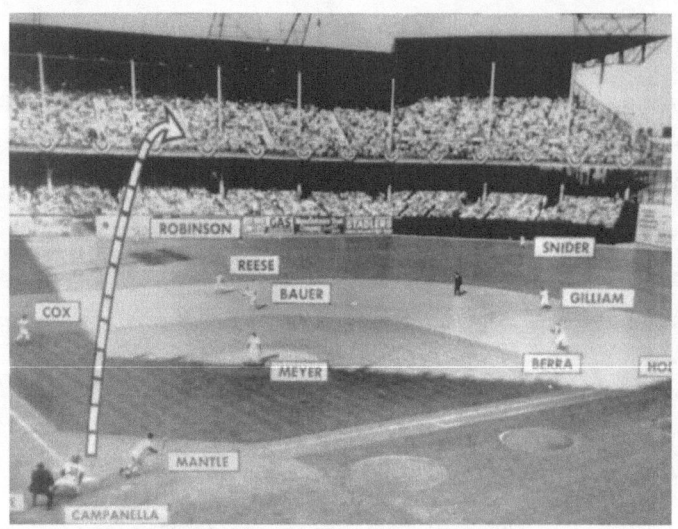

*This was Mickey Mantle's 1953 World Series Game 5 Grand Slam Home Run against the Brooklyn Dodgers.*

*The 1964 World Series Game 3: Mantle's home run in the bottom of the 9th inning beats the Cardinals 2-1. Barney Schultz, the dejected Cardinal Pitcher, walks off the field as 3rd base coach Frank Crosetti congratulates mantle.*

*Mickey Mantle's catch in Game 5 of the 1956 World Series preserved Don Larson's perfect game. Mantle also hit a home run in the 2-0 win.*

*Reflections Part I*

*Mitch Ryder and the Detroit Wheels in 1964. Two years later, they released "Devil with the Blue Dress On."*

*A Mitch Ryder and the Detroit Wheels "Breakout" album was Kenny's all-time favorite.*

*Kenny Harmon's High School Girlfriend, Pat Roberts, crowned Basketball Queen*

*Kenny Harmon*

## *Baltimore Colts vs. New York Giants*
### *December 28, 1958*
### *The greatest game ever played!*

*Johnny Unitas, left, in sudden-death overtime of the 1958 NFL championship game.*

*Baltimore Colts kicker Steve Myhra (65) makes a field goal with 10 seconds remaining in the game against the New York Giants to tie the score. The game went into overtime, and the Colts captured the 1958 NFL championship with the 23-17 victory.*

74-year-old Curns Harmon holding his grandsons, Billy & Glenn Harmon, at Dibble in 1929.

Curns Harman when he lived in Liberty, Missouri before he moved to Verden, Oklahoma. This was before he began spelling his name "Harmon."

Seventeen-year-old Kenny Harmon in November 1967, with his '65 Impala.

*Kenneth Swinney standing next to Cecil Harmon who is holding Glenn Harmon with Billy Harmon standing in front (1931)*

*Kenny's cousins Nedra, Raymond, and Paula Swinney in 1953.*

*Date night with Pat Roberts at the Washita Theater in Chickasha, Spring 1968*

# The Sad Papaw Books

Kenny Harmon has lived a life full of the ups and downs that many of us face. There was dating, friends, family, and high school fun, along with facing fears, broken relationships, and financial struggles. He also saw the dark side of life, the death of a brother, then the death of a friend, and backbreaking work as a teenager. Those trials, all the good and the bad, shaped the man he is today. He grew to be a hardworking man who loves his family; practices his faith, and honors our soldiers. The man who today is known around the world as Sad Papaw has chosen to share his life with the rest of us. As we all wondered who is the man behind the sad tweet, he now regales us with what life taught him and what he can now teach us. It begins with the importance of family. As you close book number two, know that he has much more to share with us as the Sad Papaw series continues.

www.ingramcontent.com/pod-product-compliance
Lightning Source LLC
LaVergne TN
LVHW041635060526
838200LV00040B/1584